I am grateful to God for everything! And I believe that the meaning of life is to make sense of other lives. C.A., you are the meaning of my life.
Lov U

Ademilton Sousa

2023

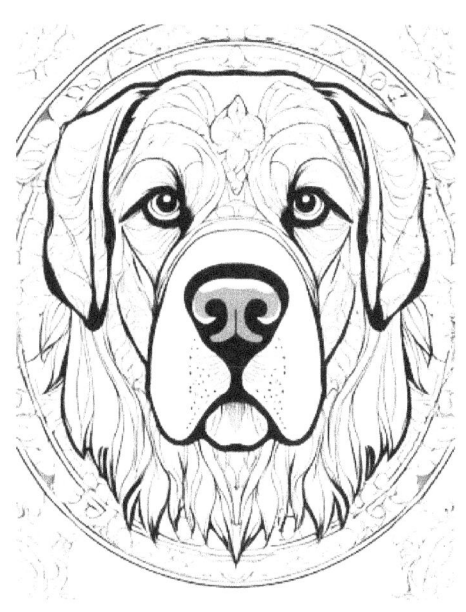
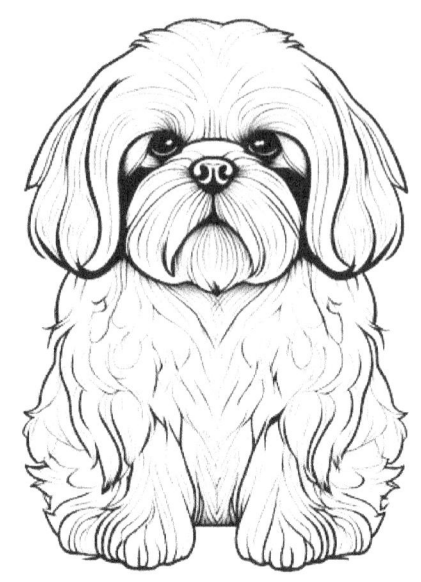

This Book Belongs to:

○━━━━━━━━━━━━━━━━━━━━━━━━━○

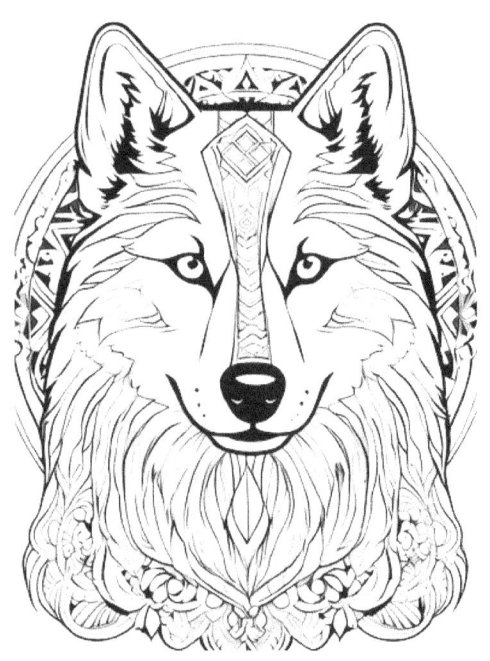

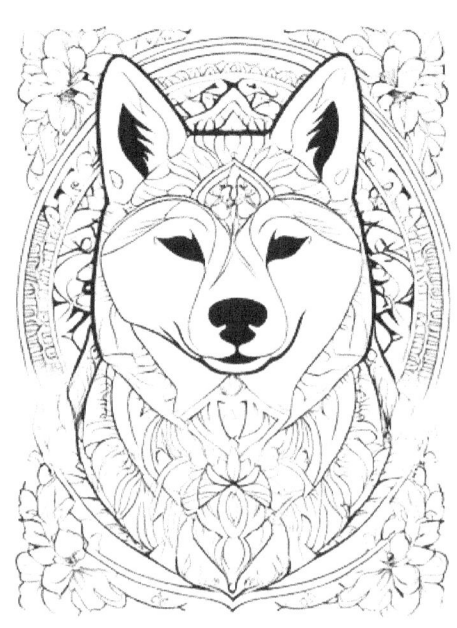

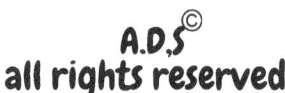

Test Color Page

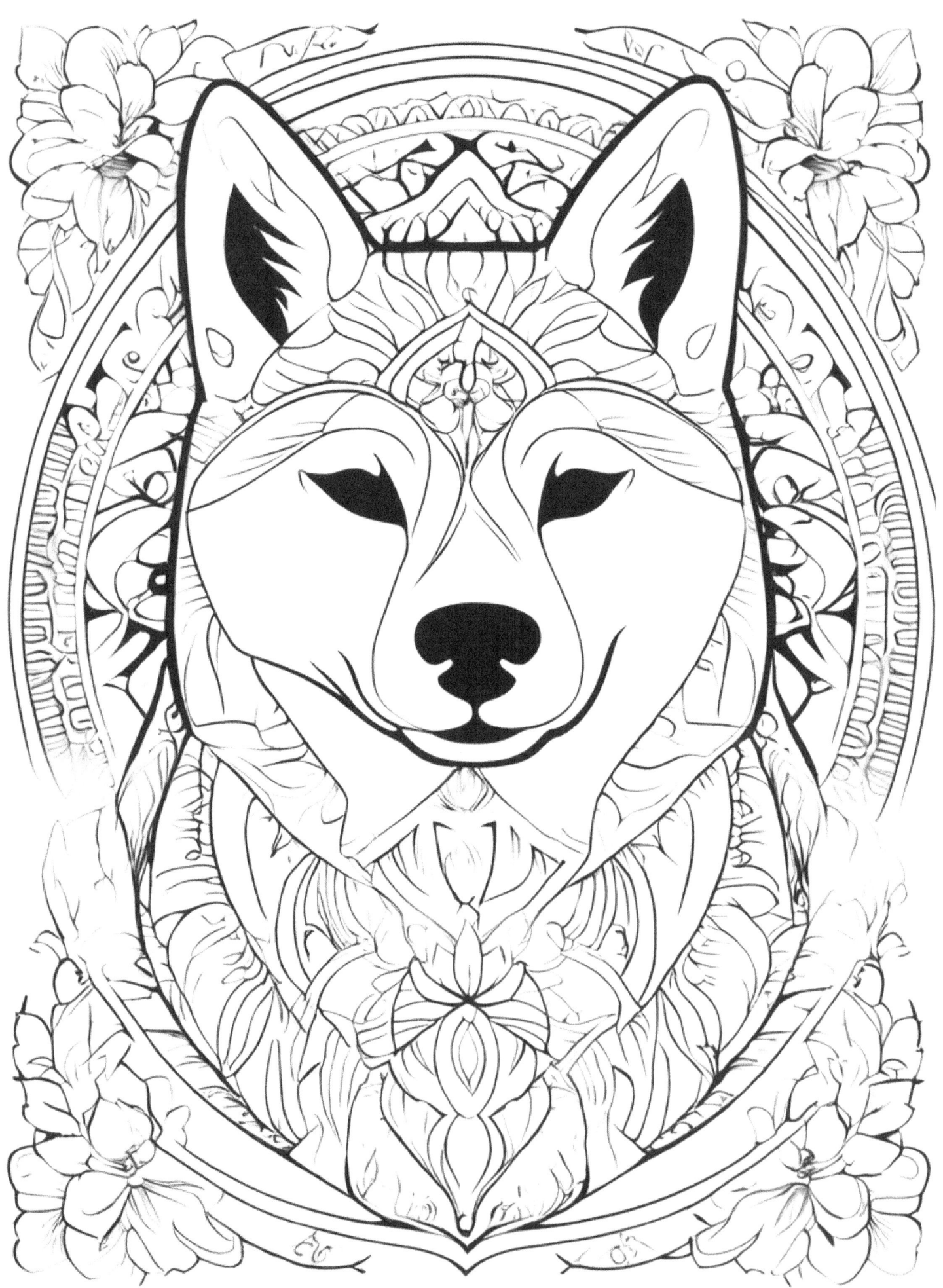

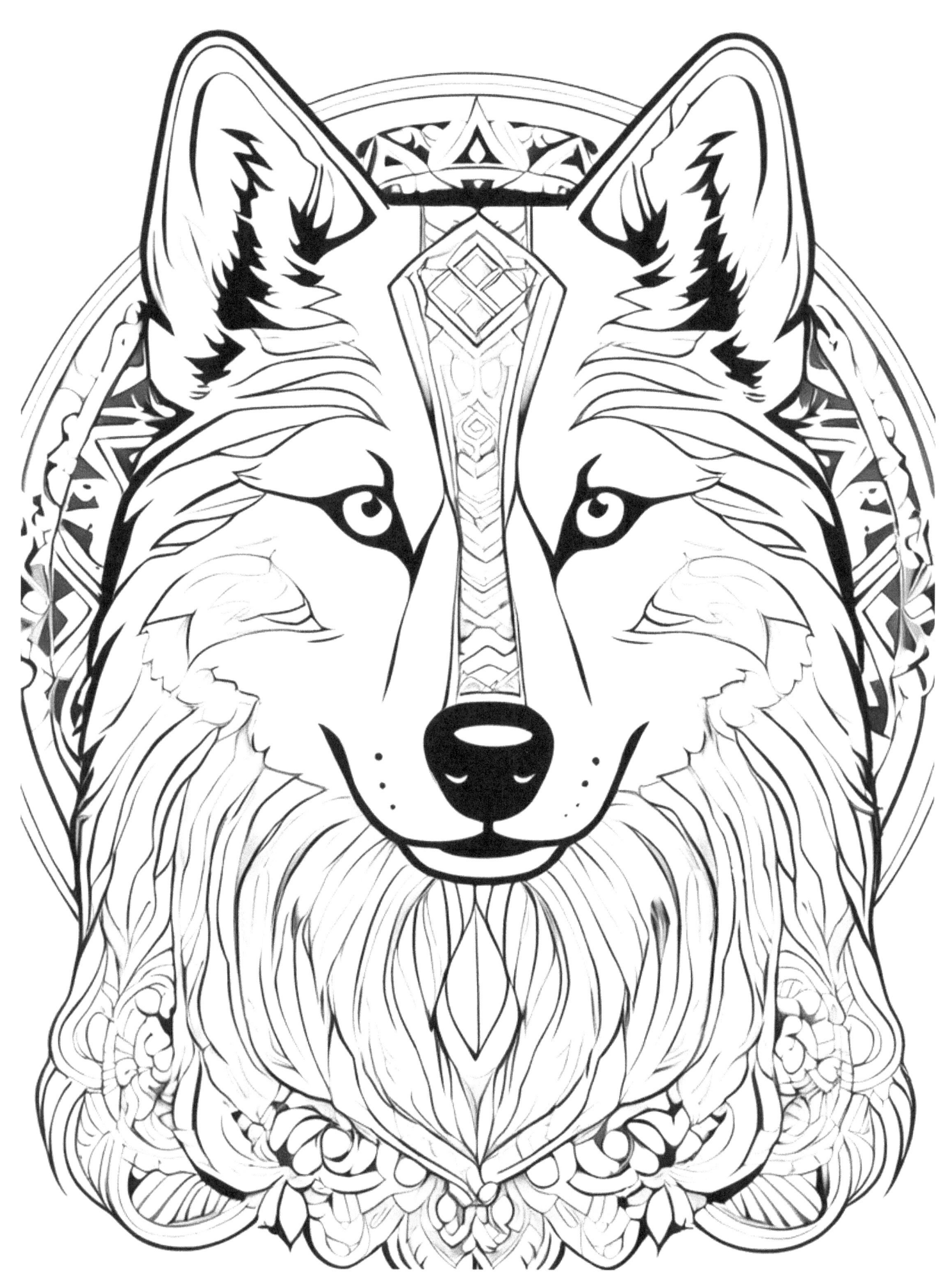

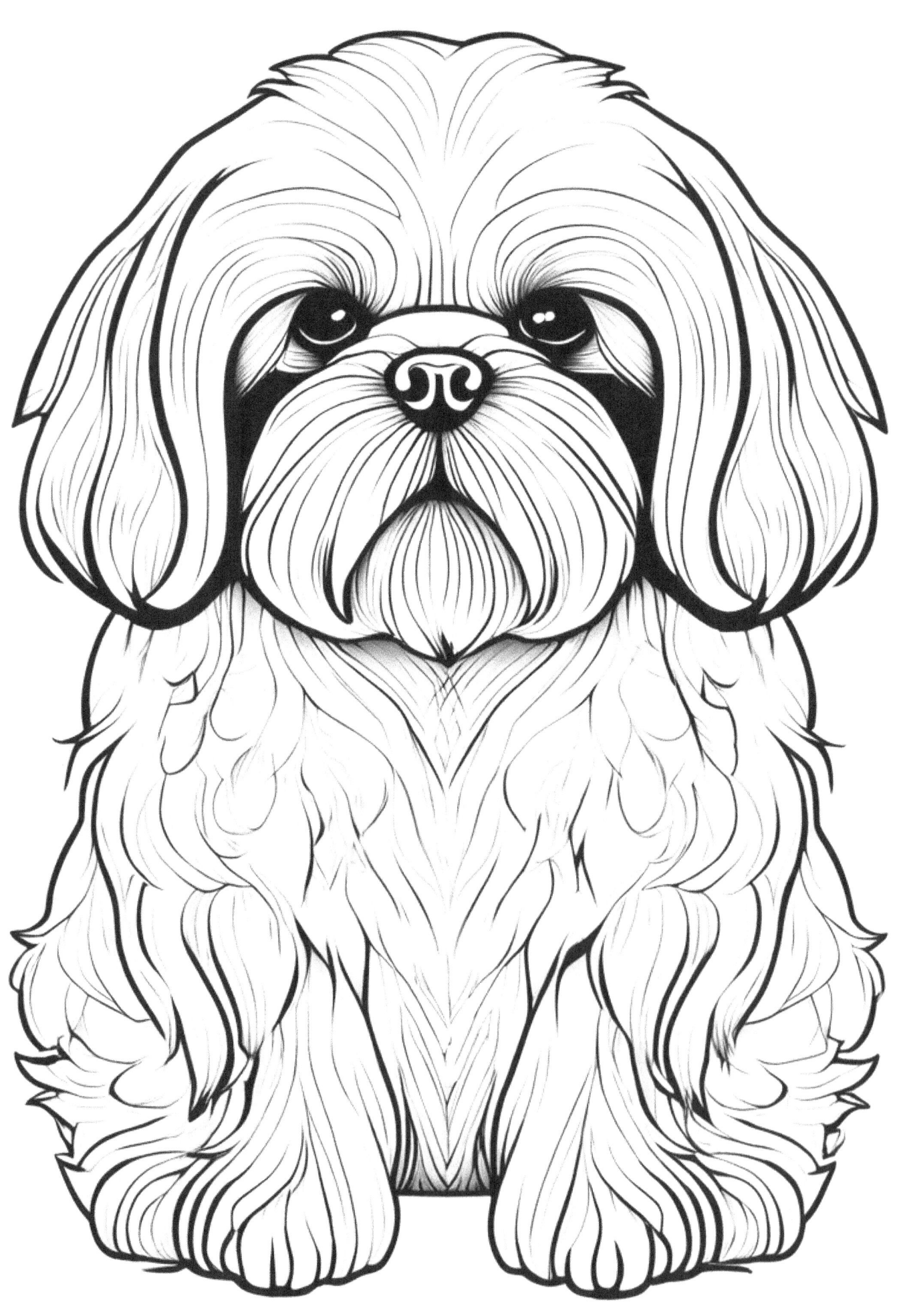

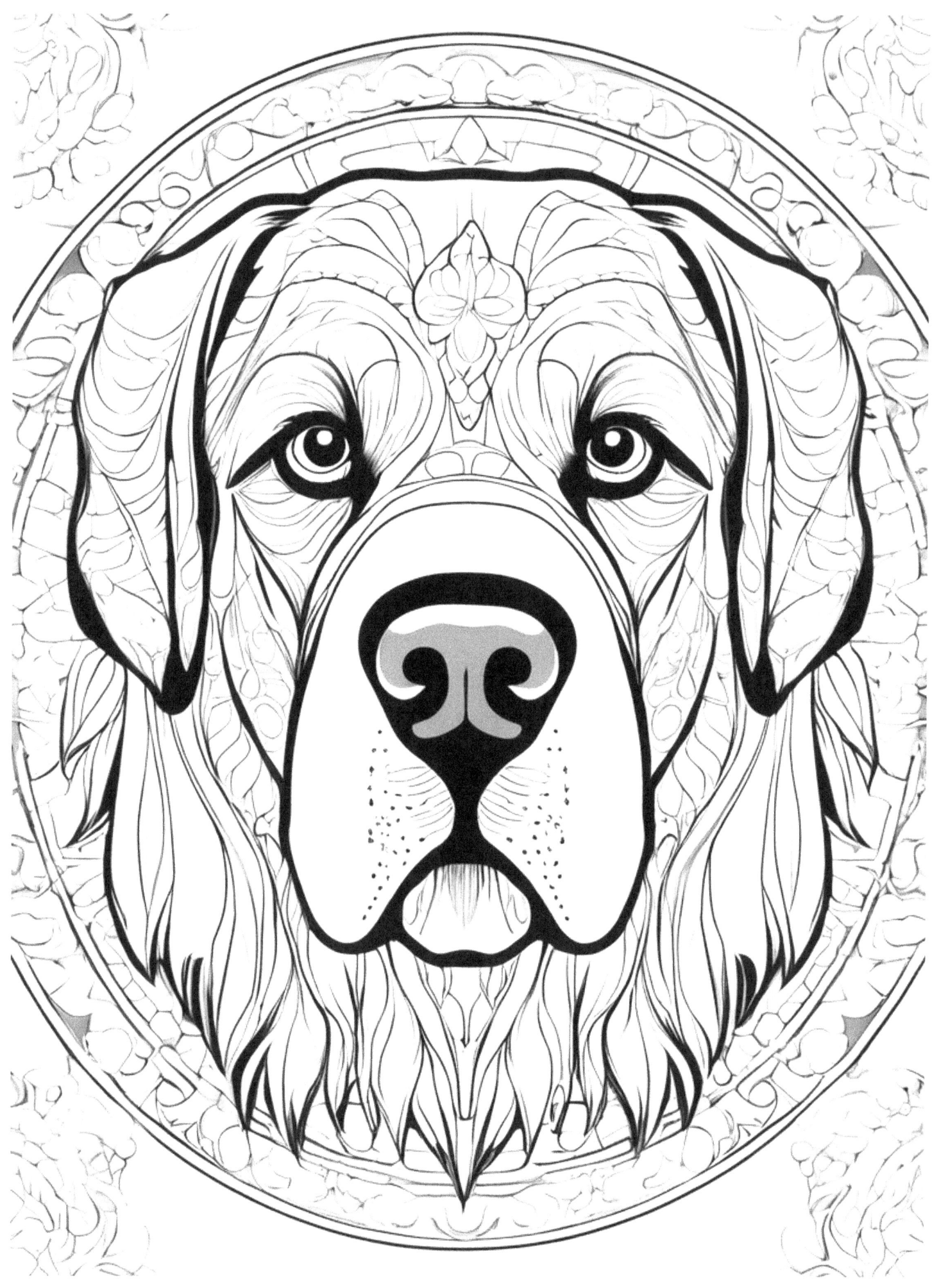

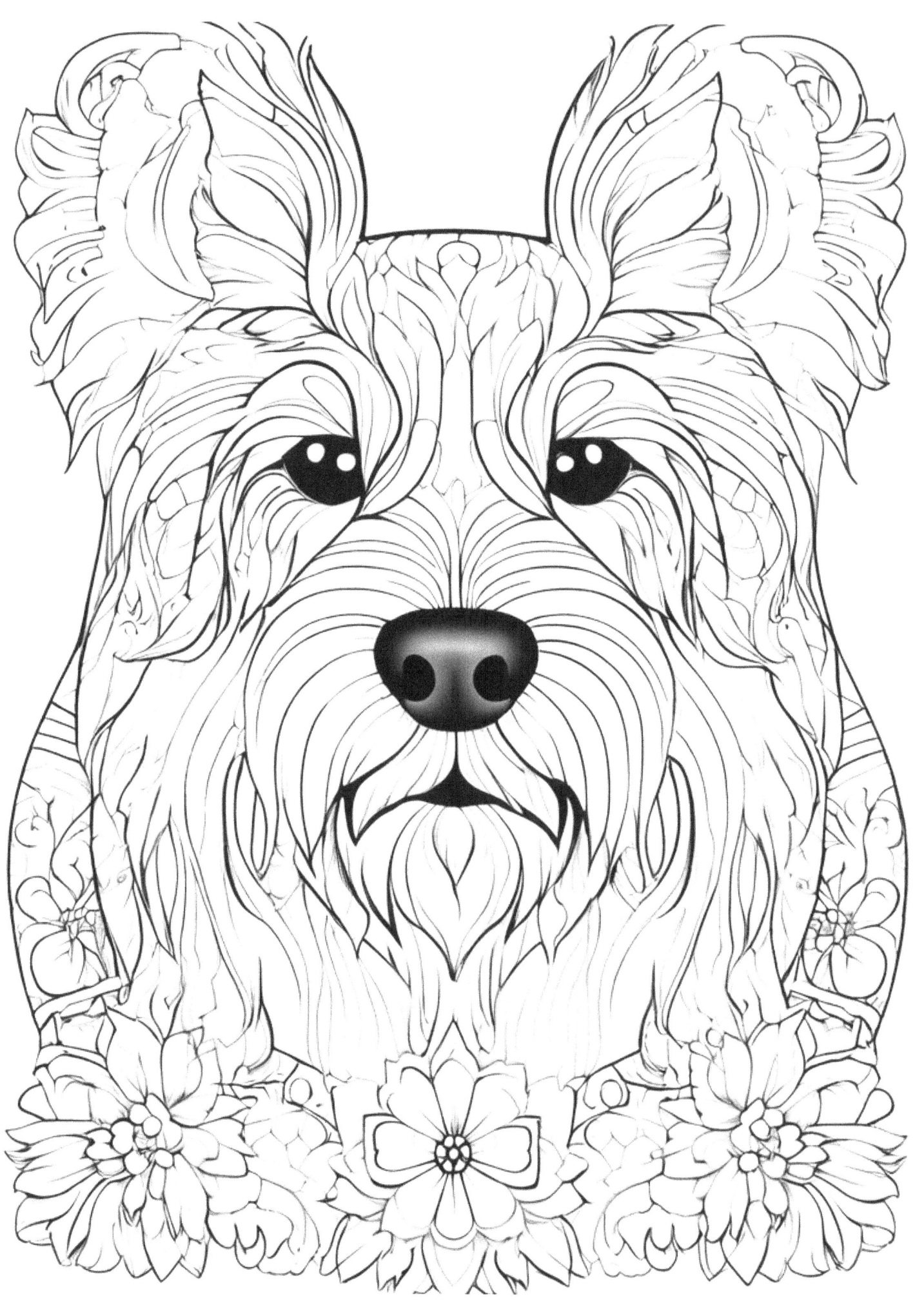

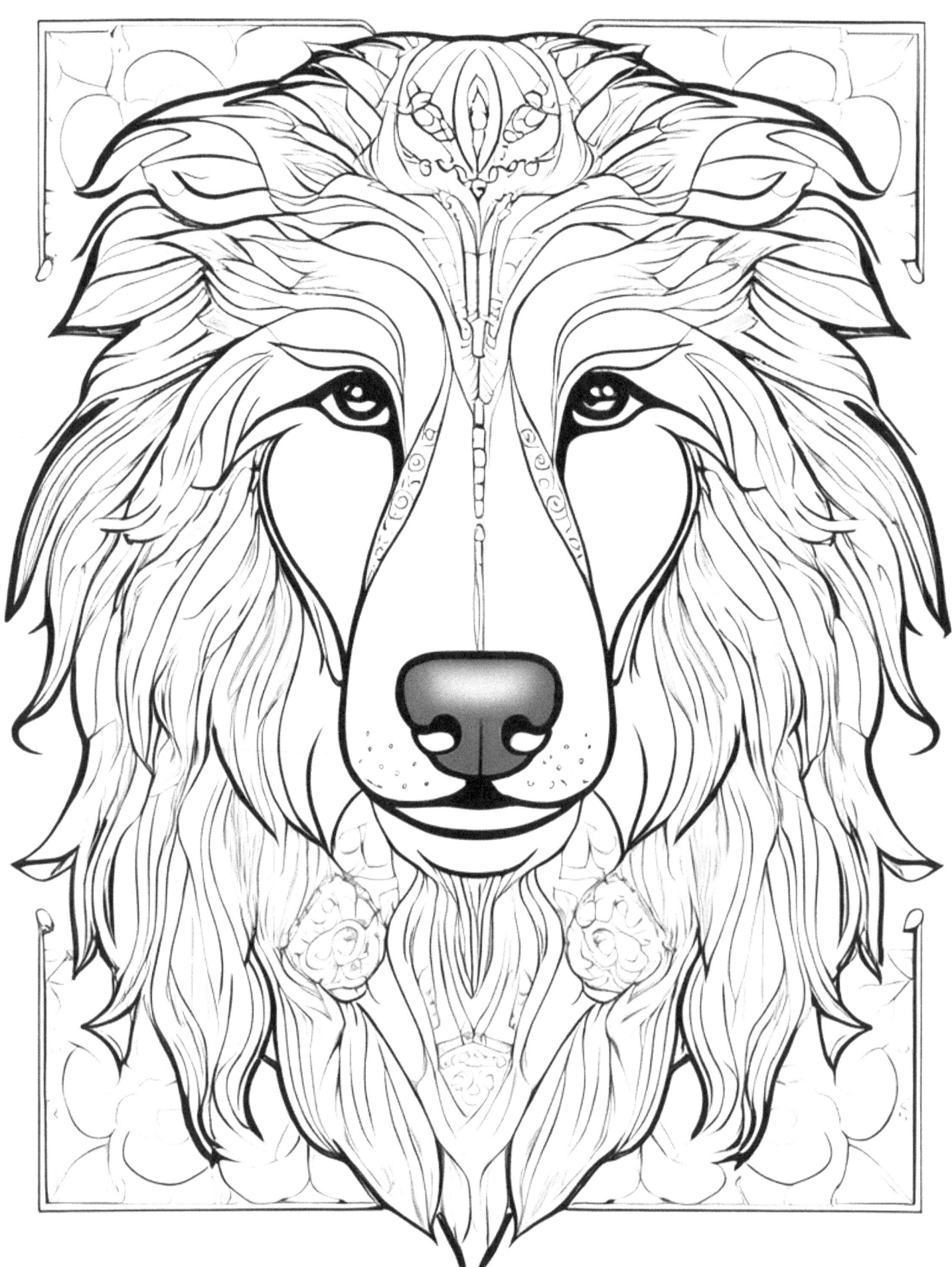

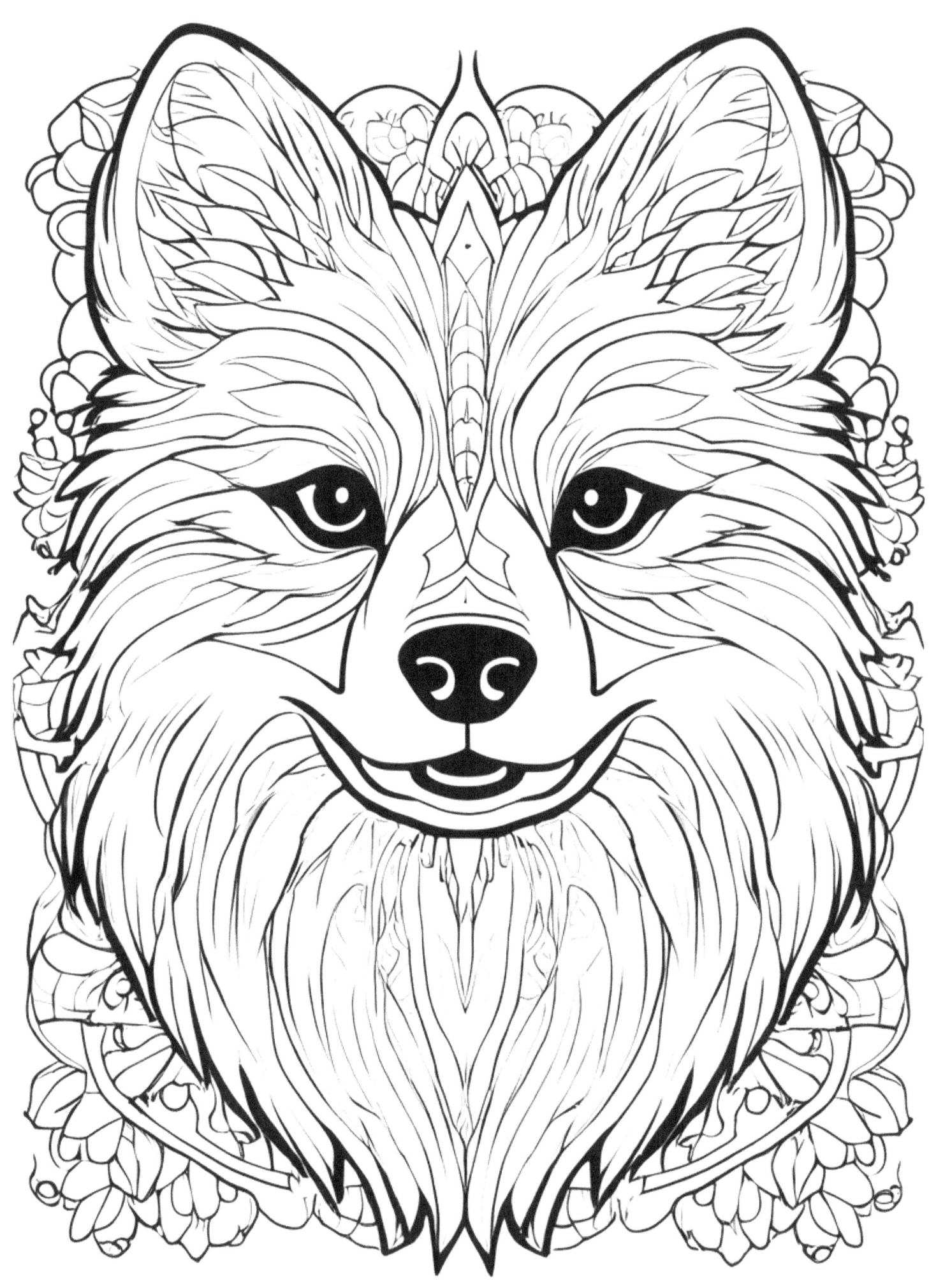

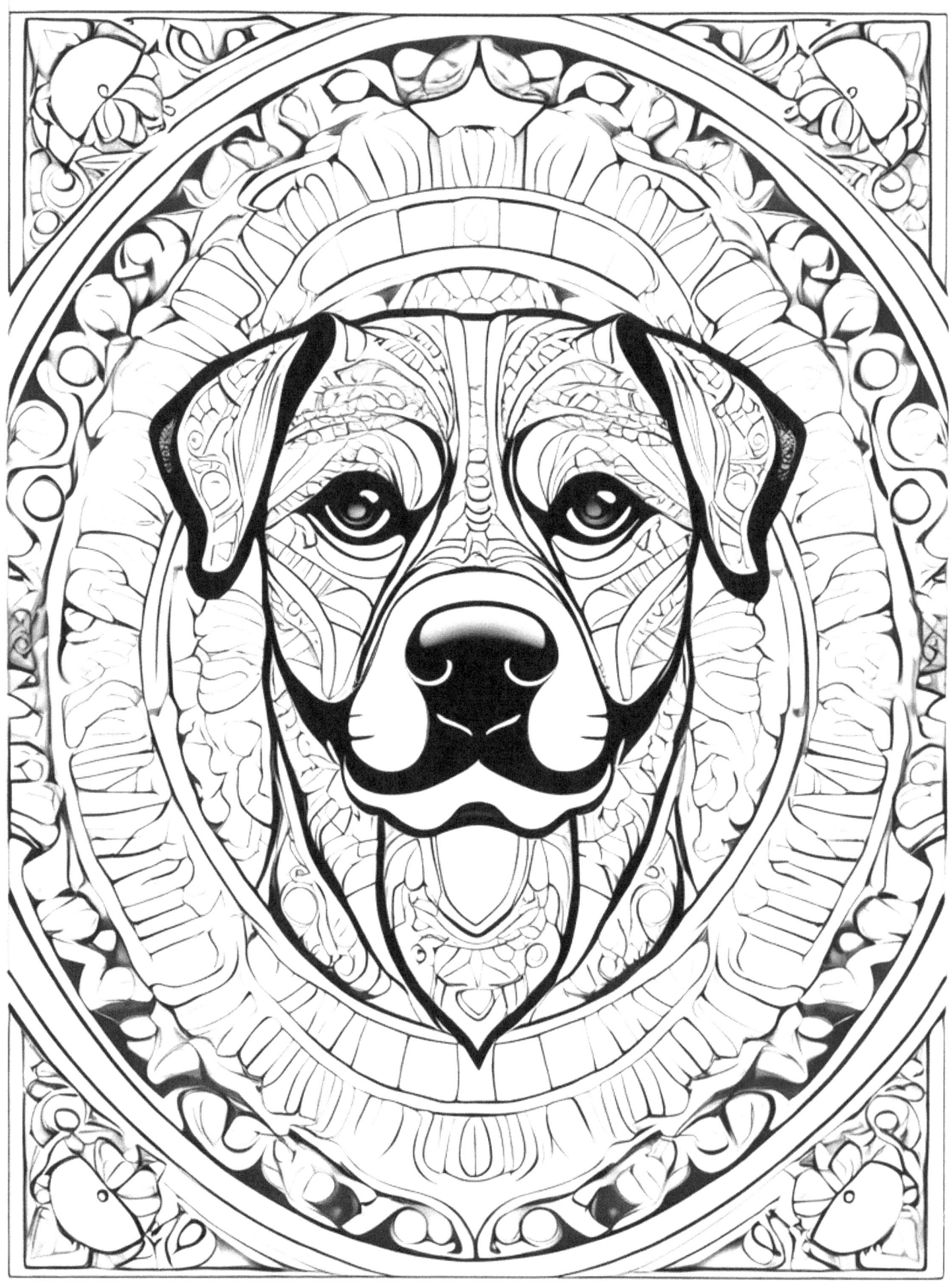

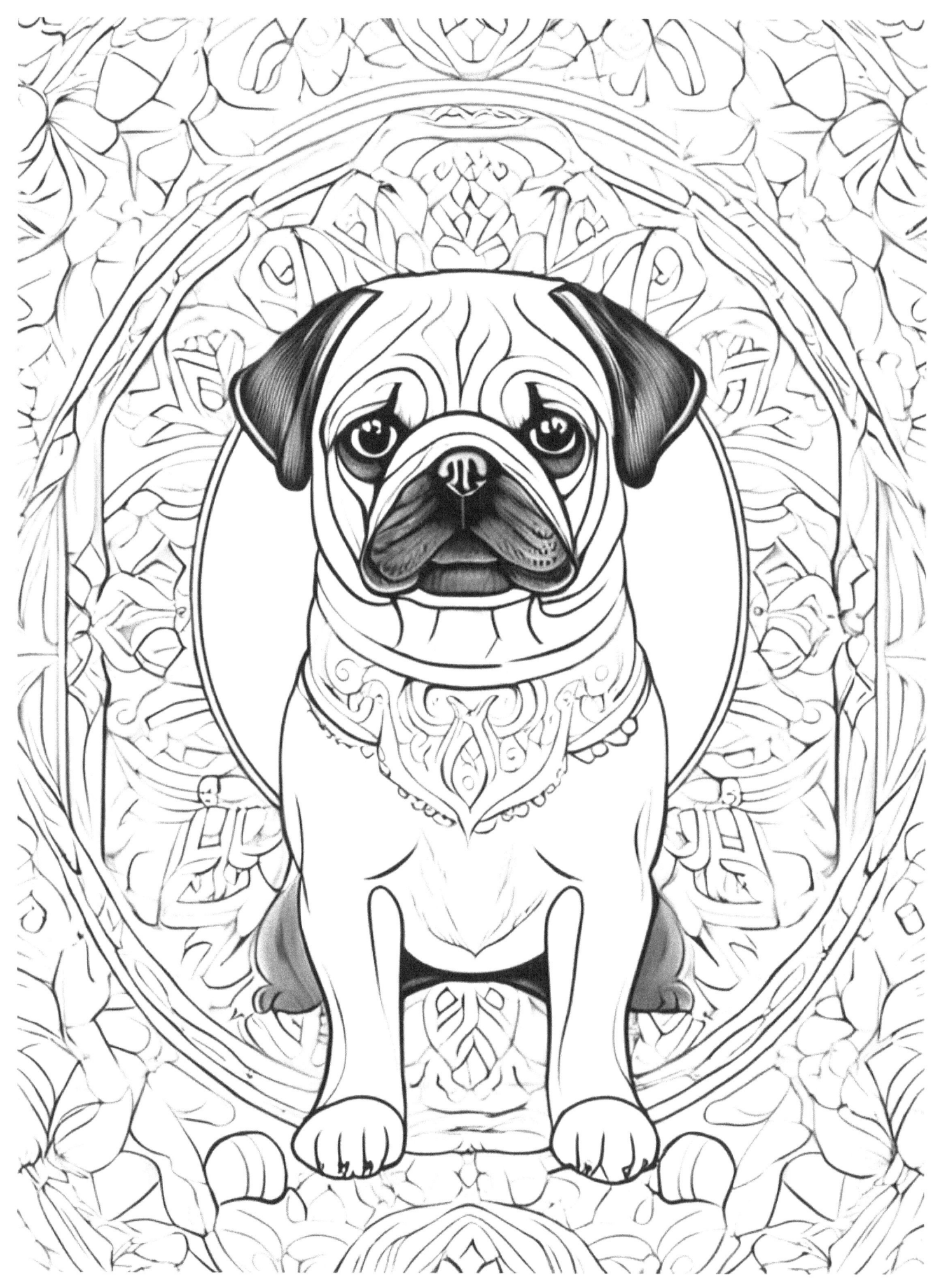

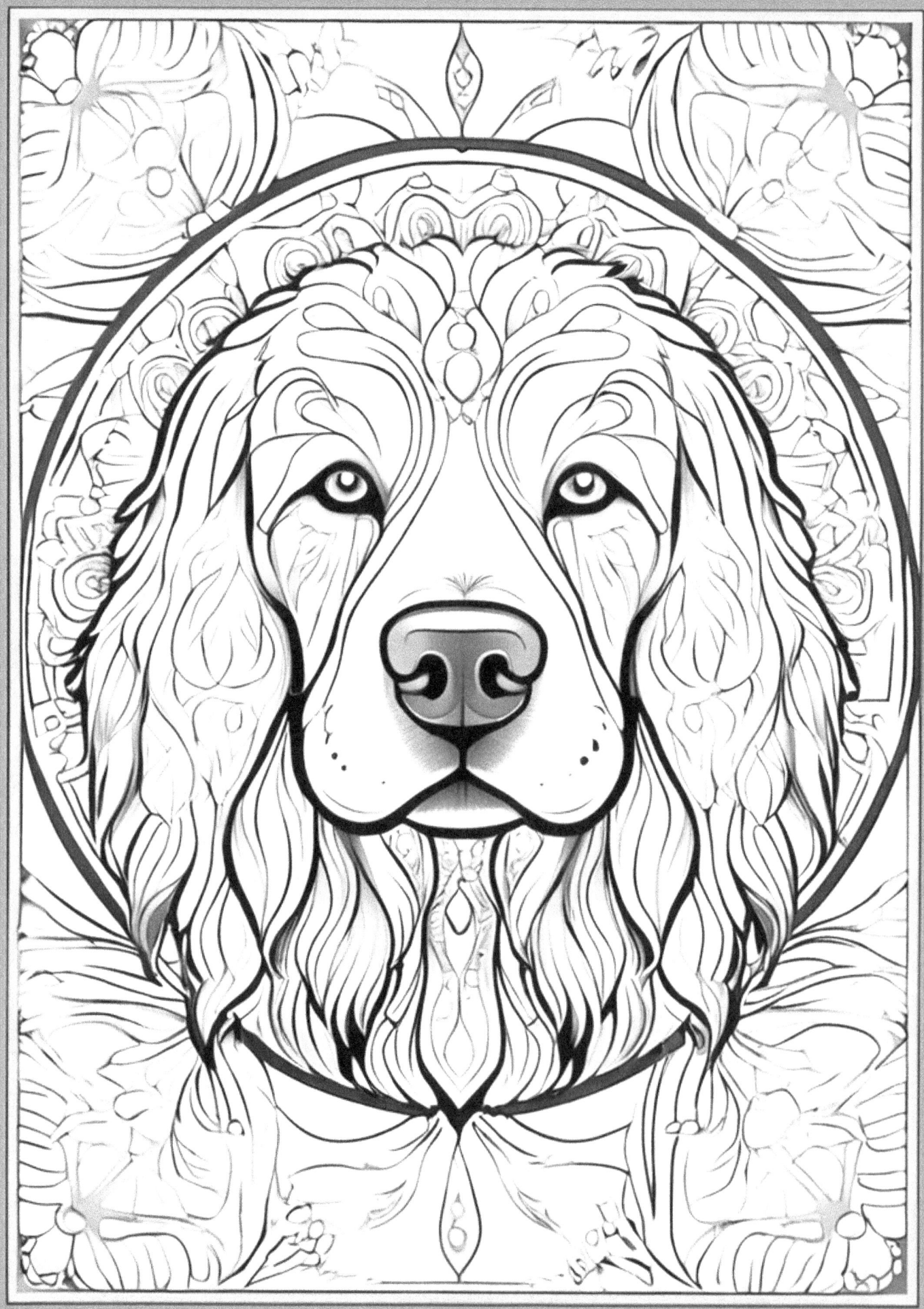

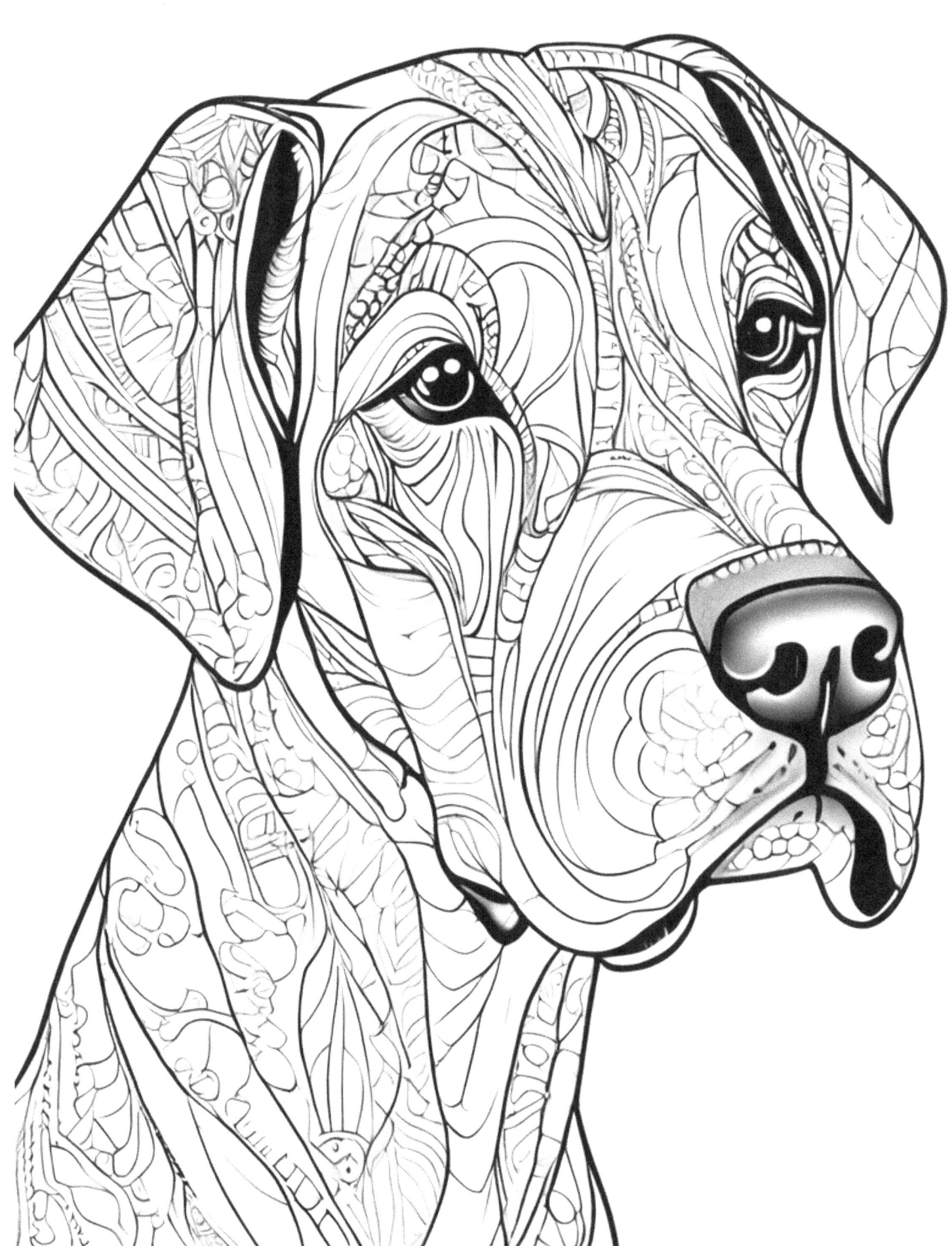

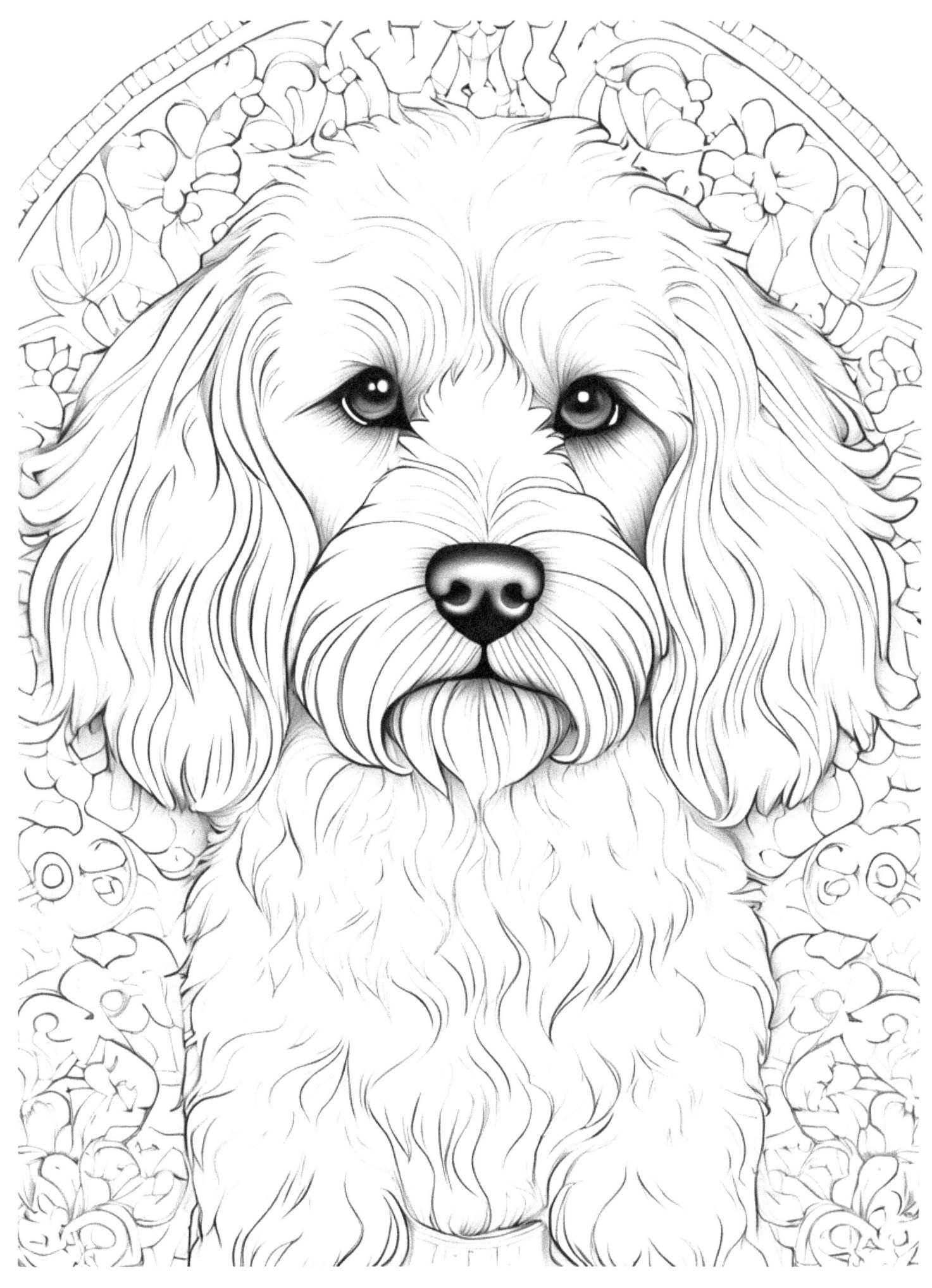

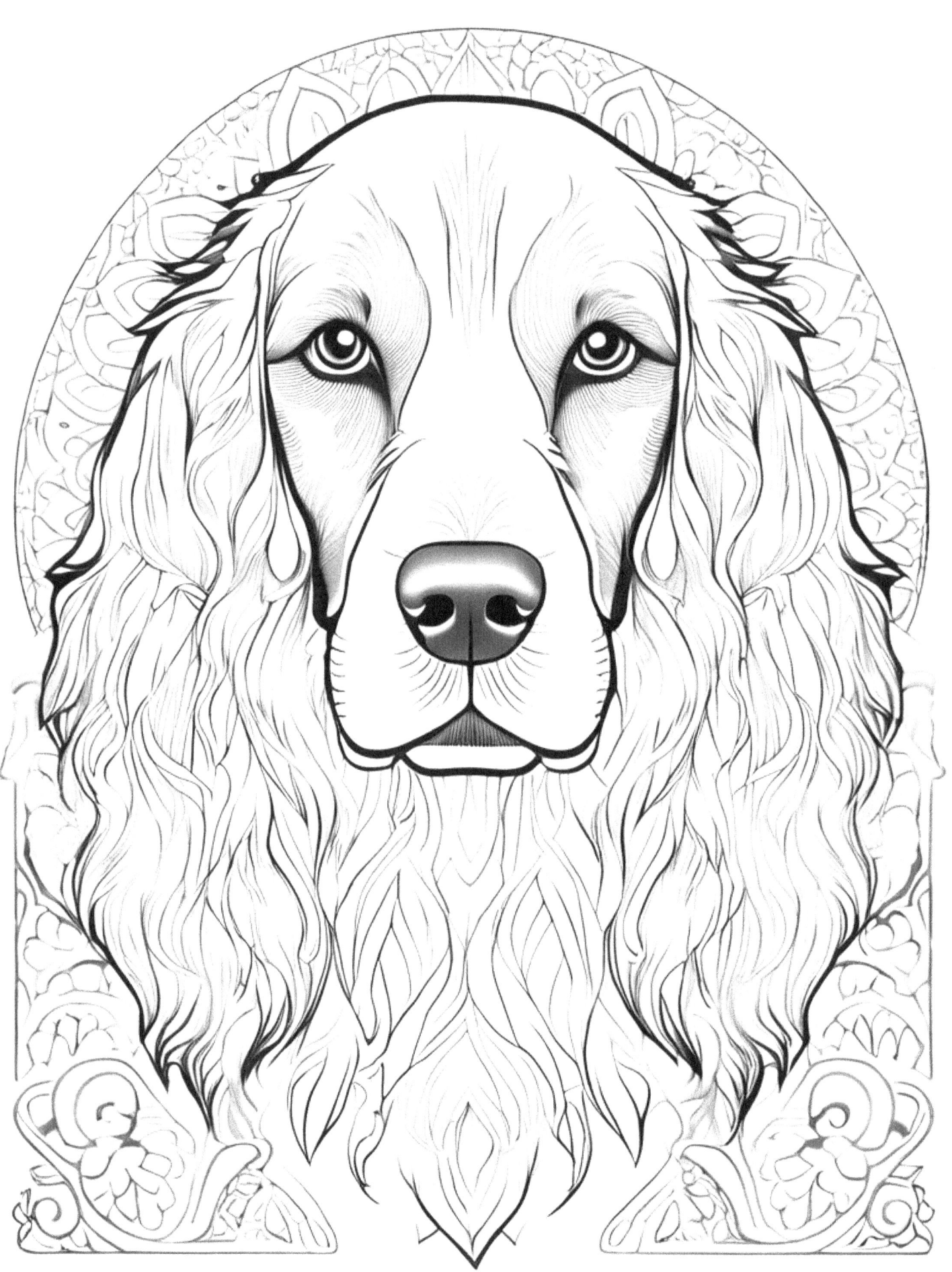

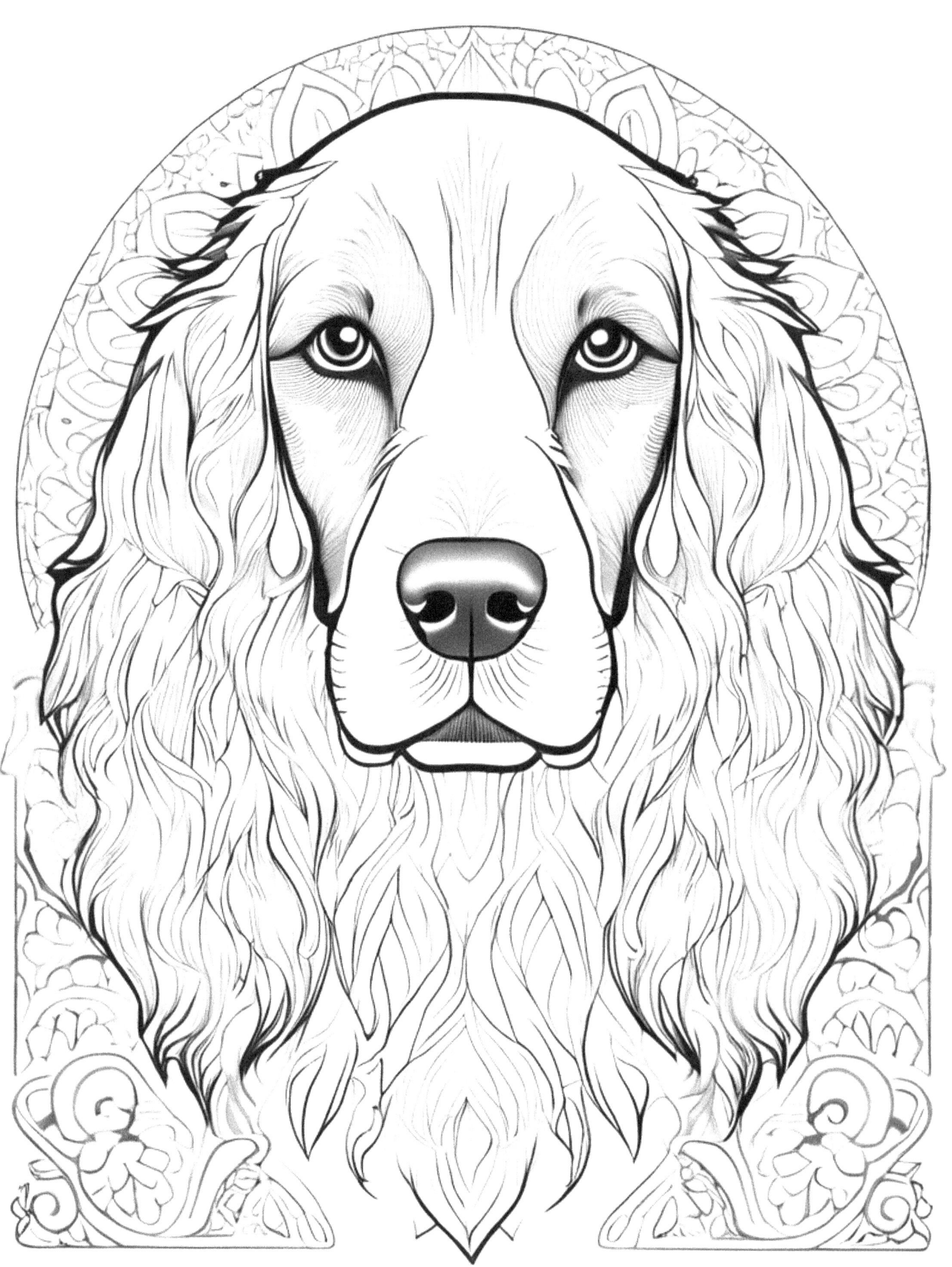

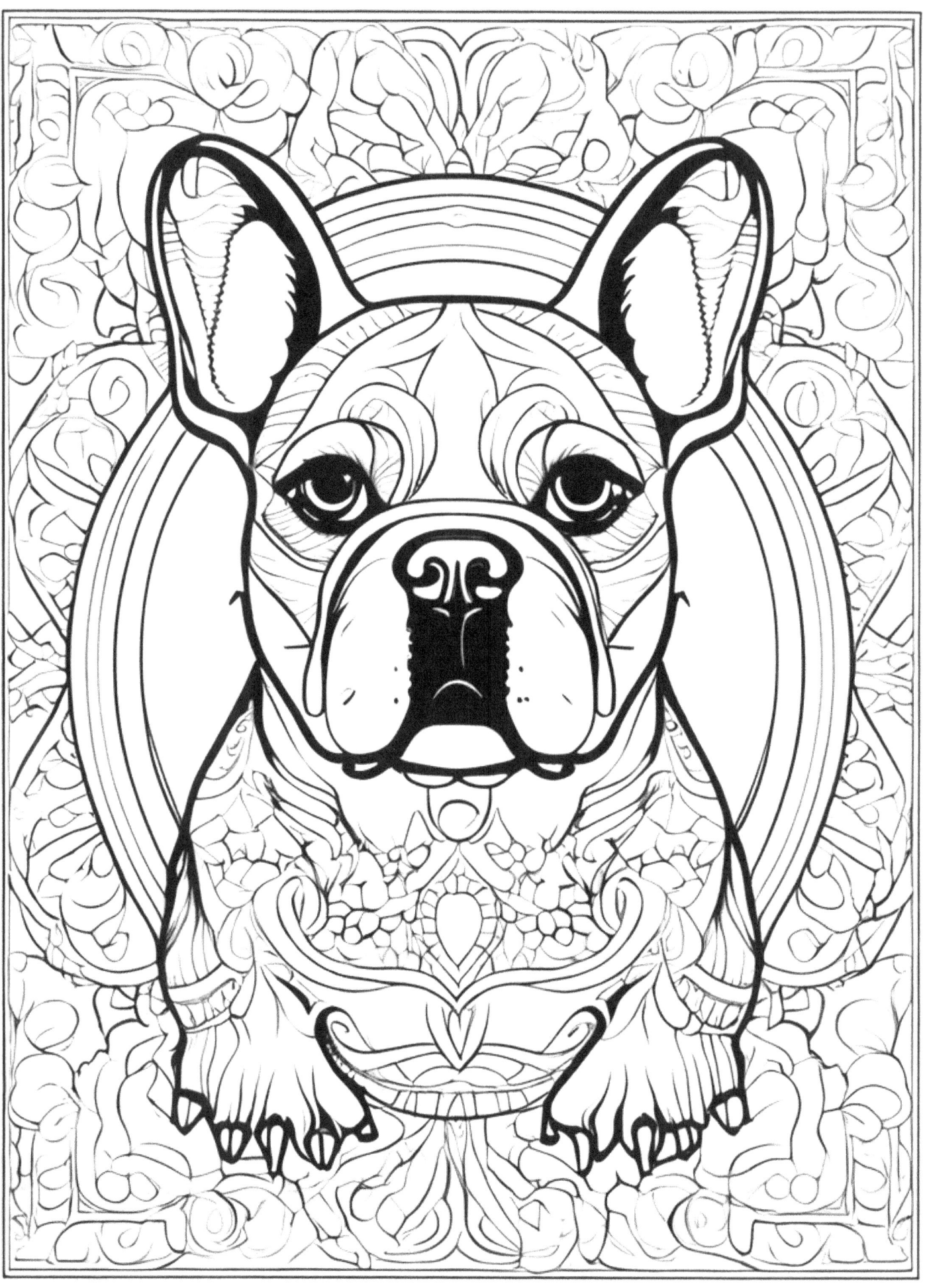

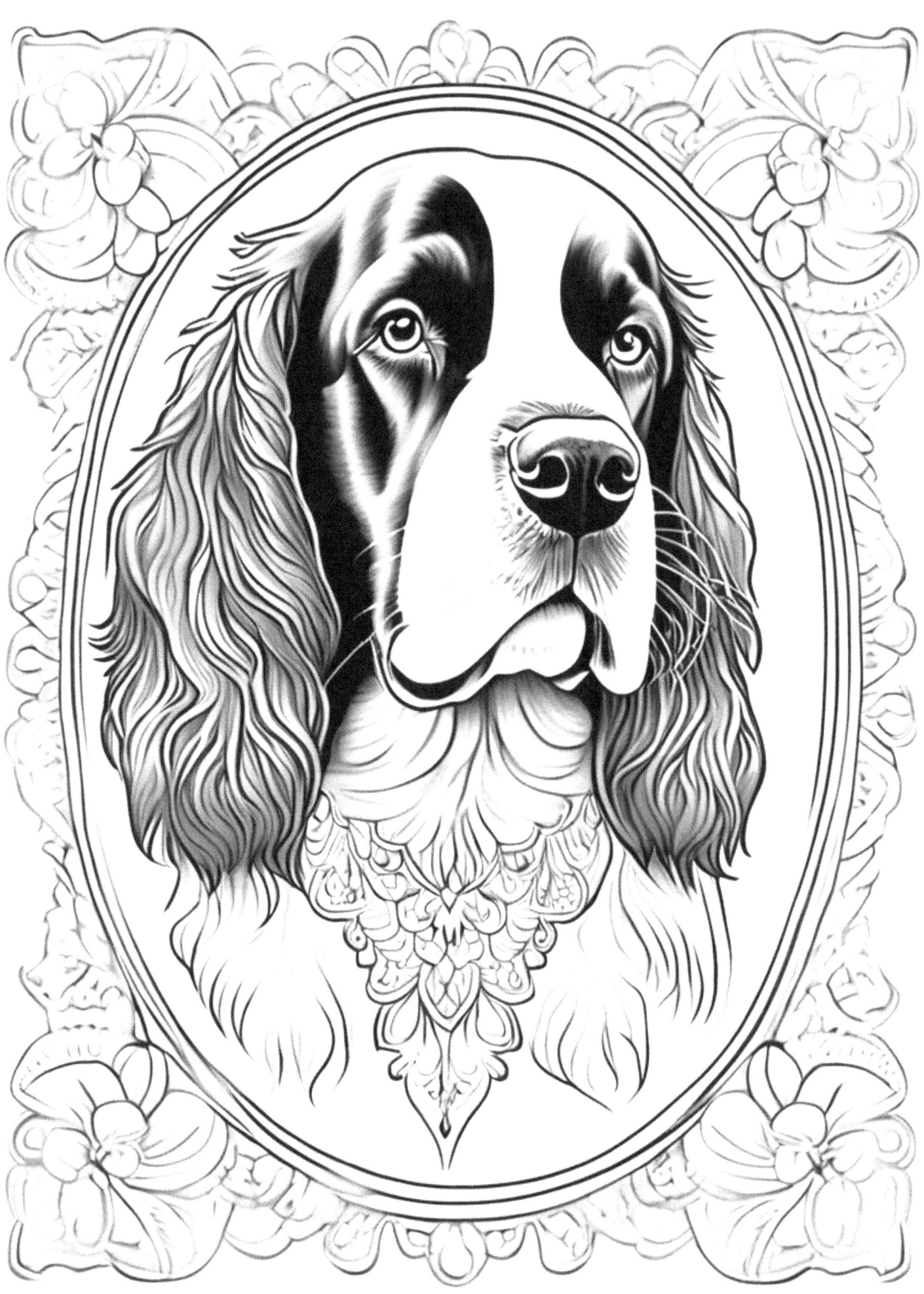

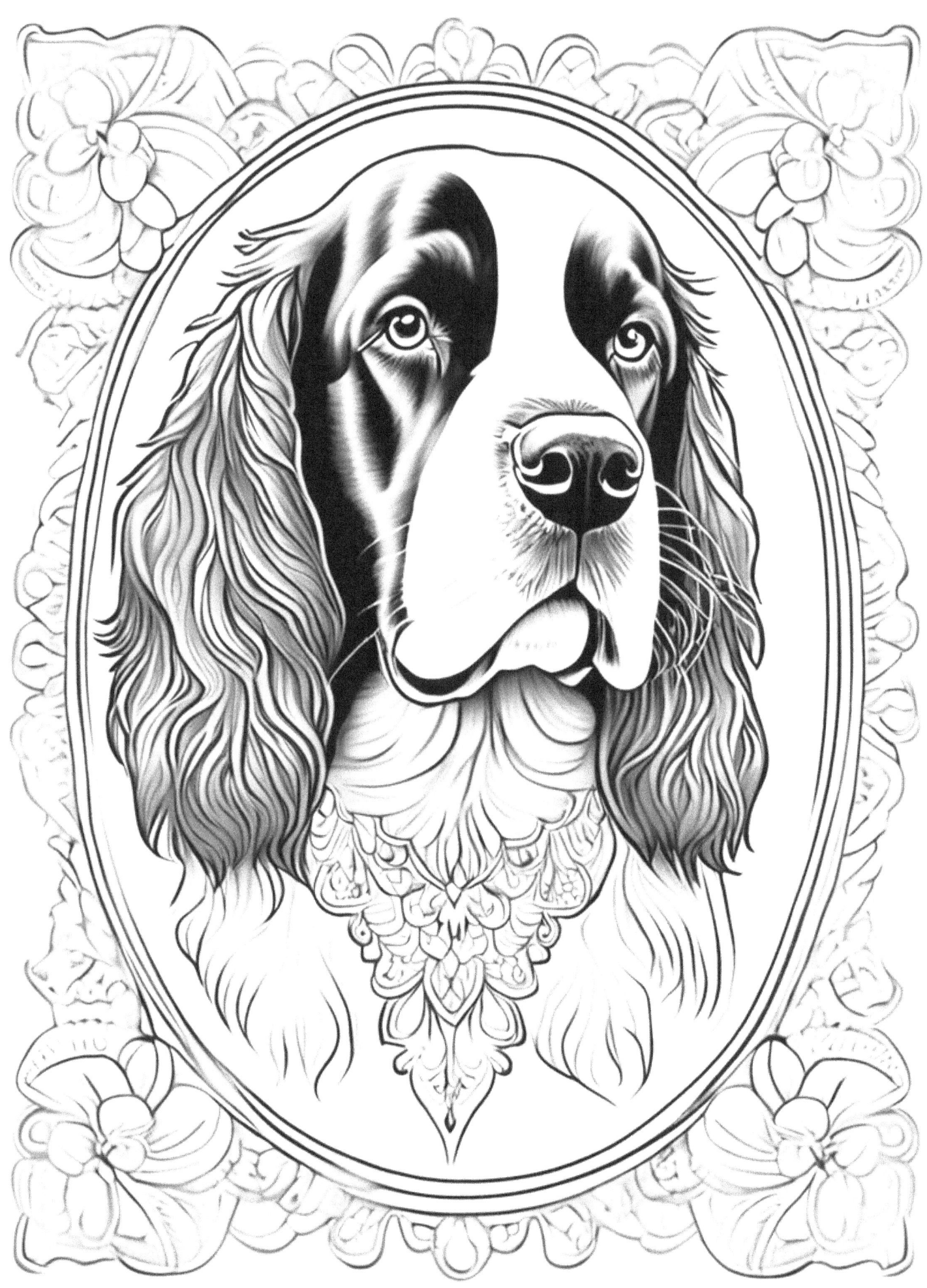

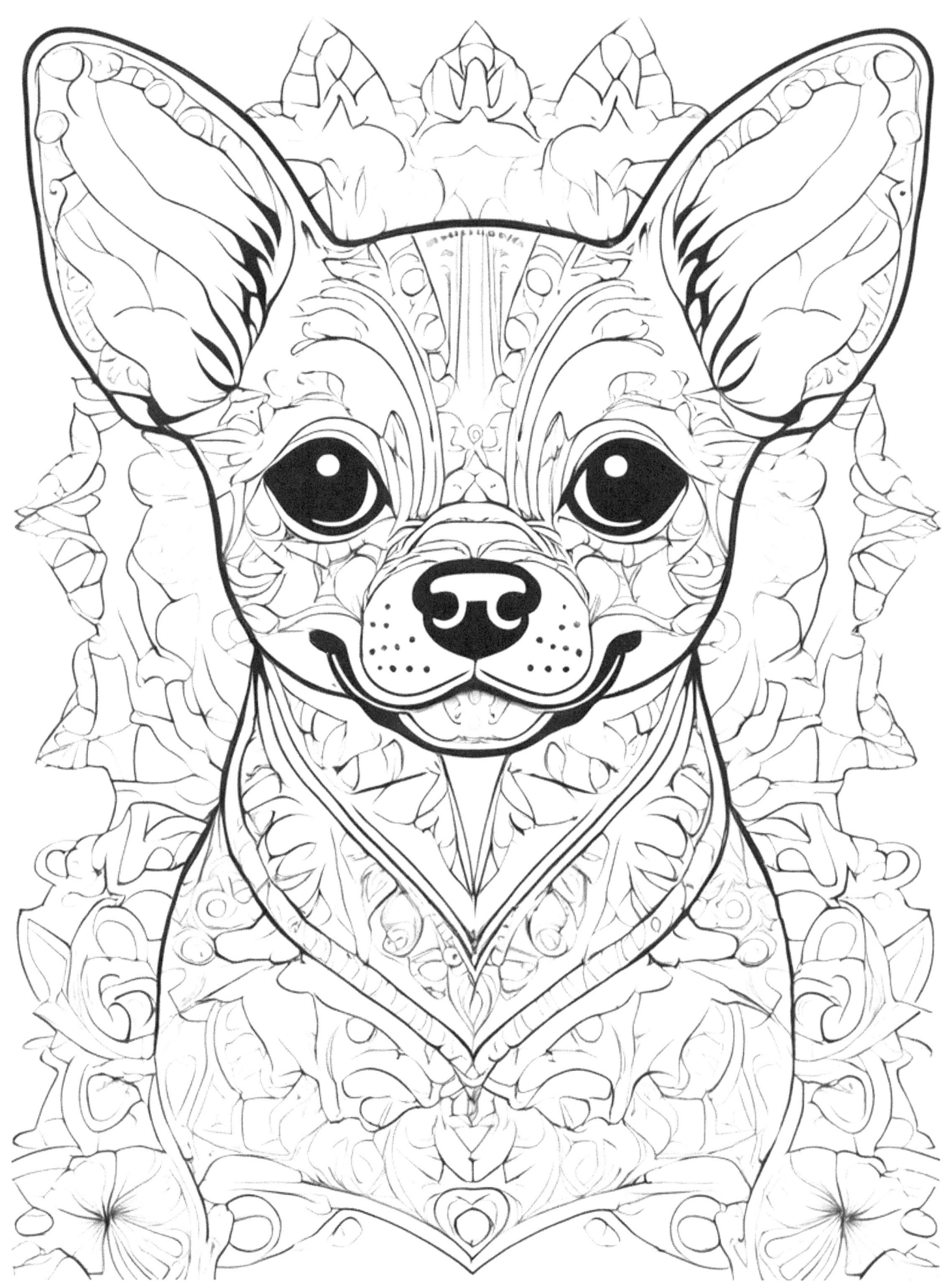

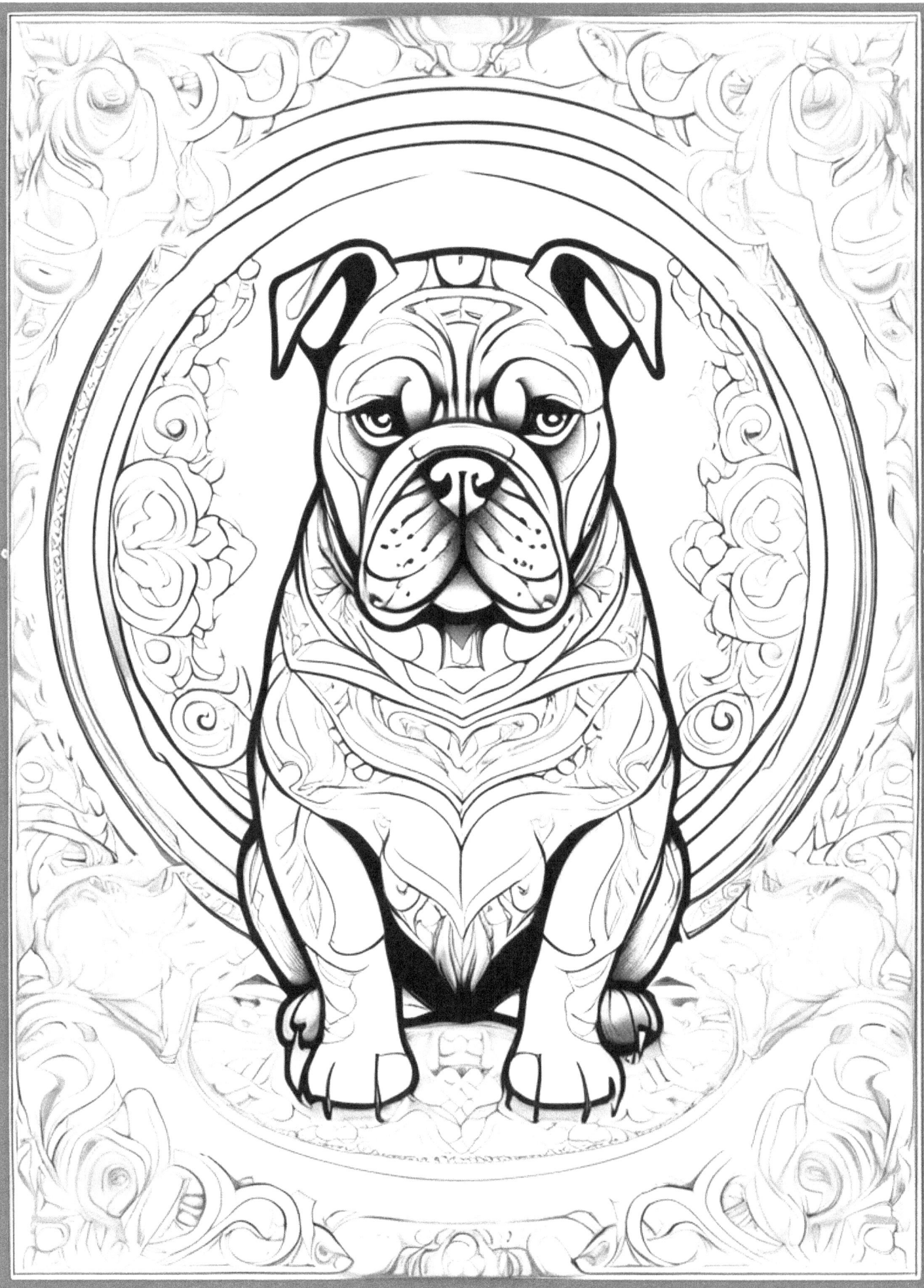

.

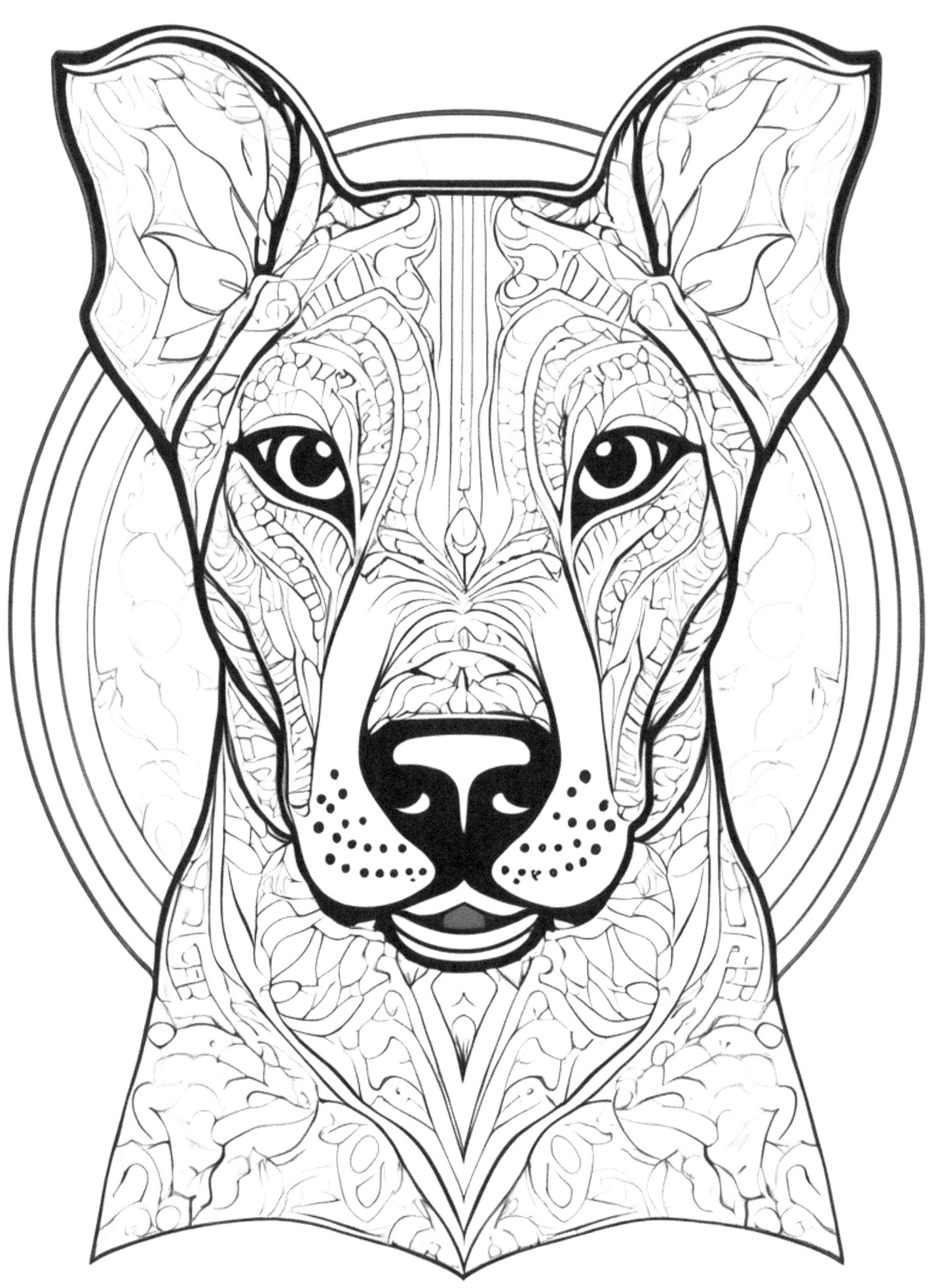

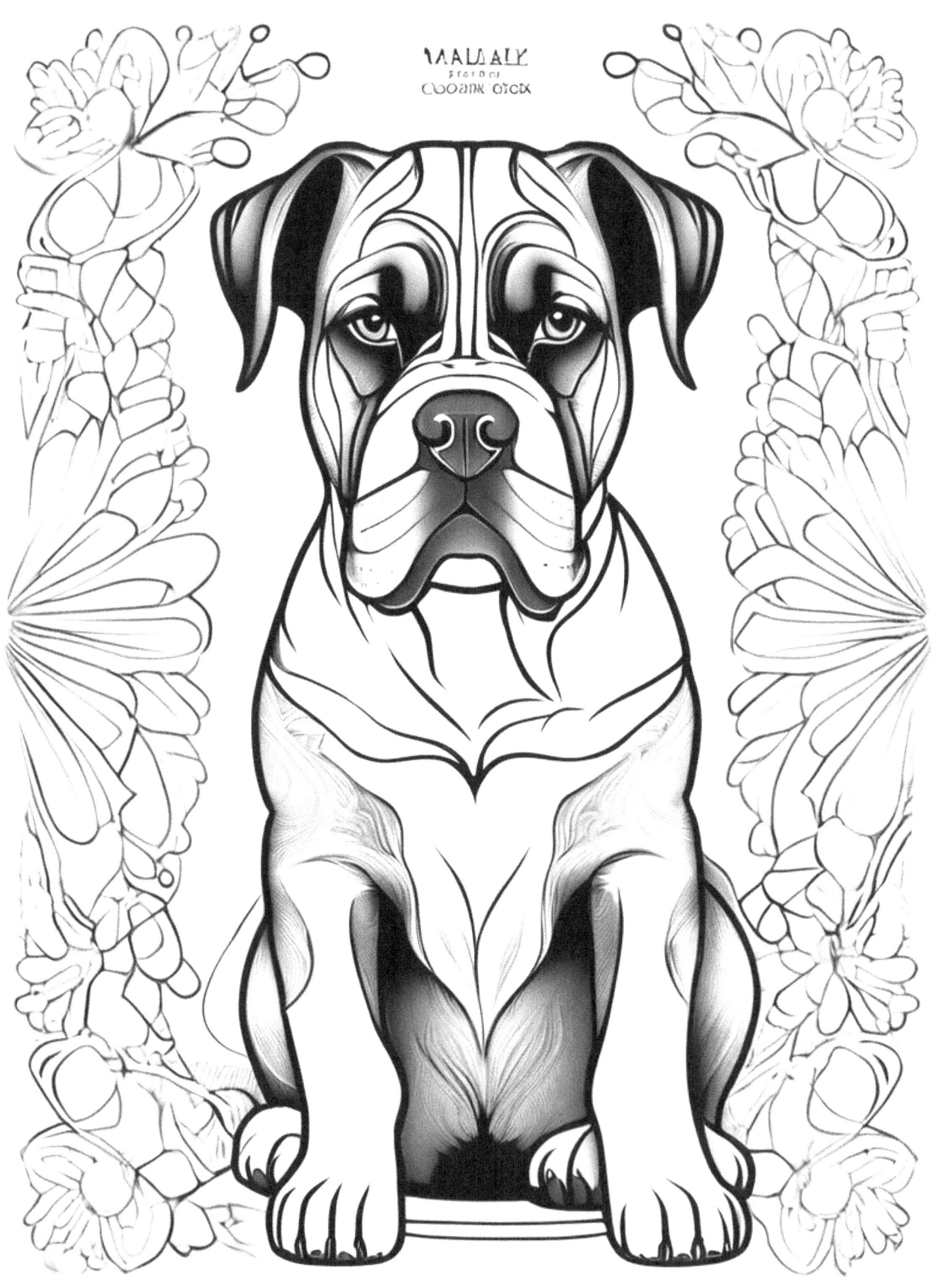

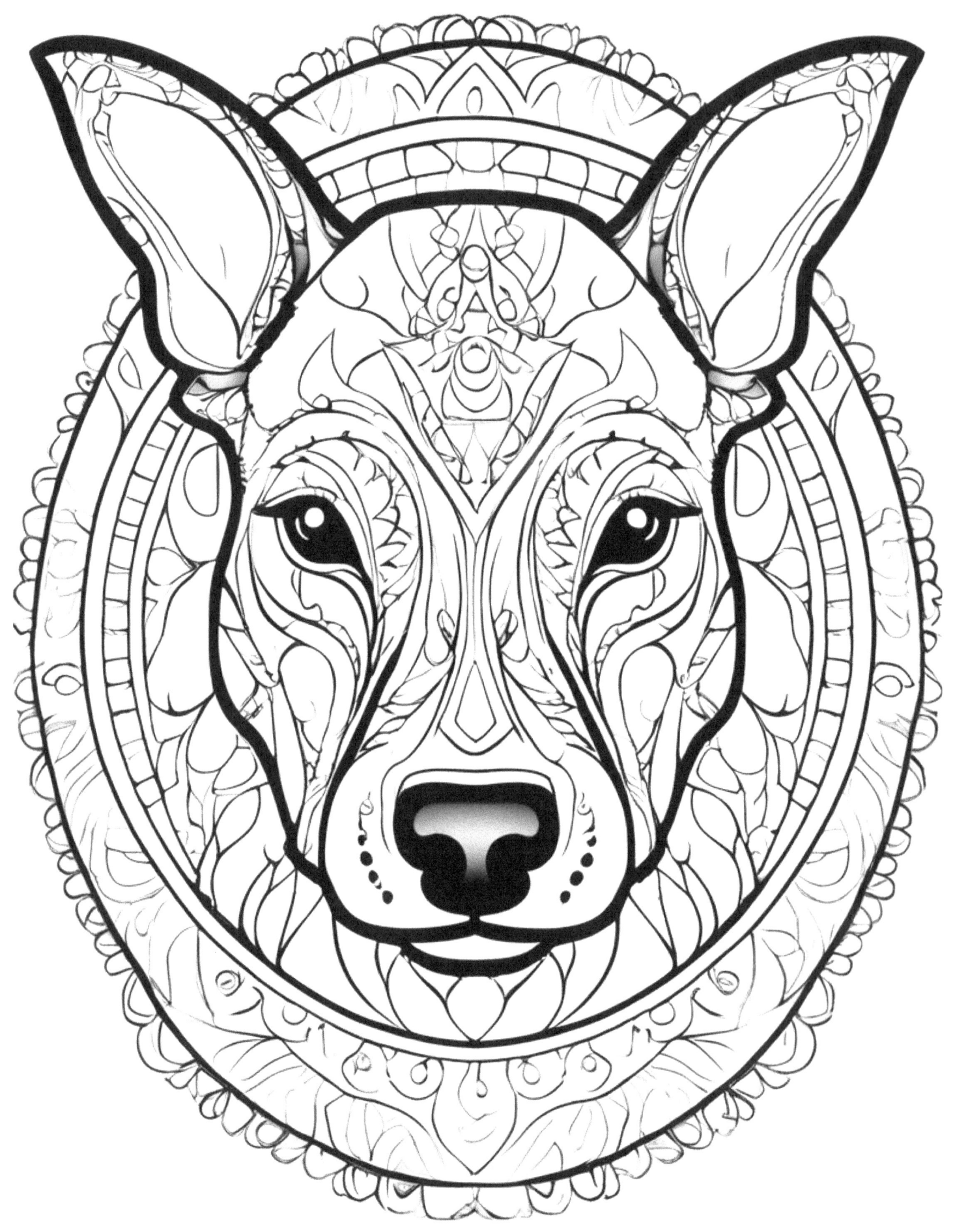

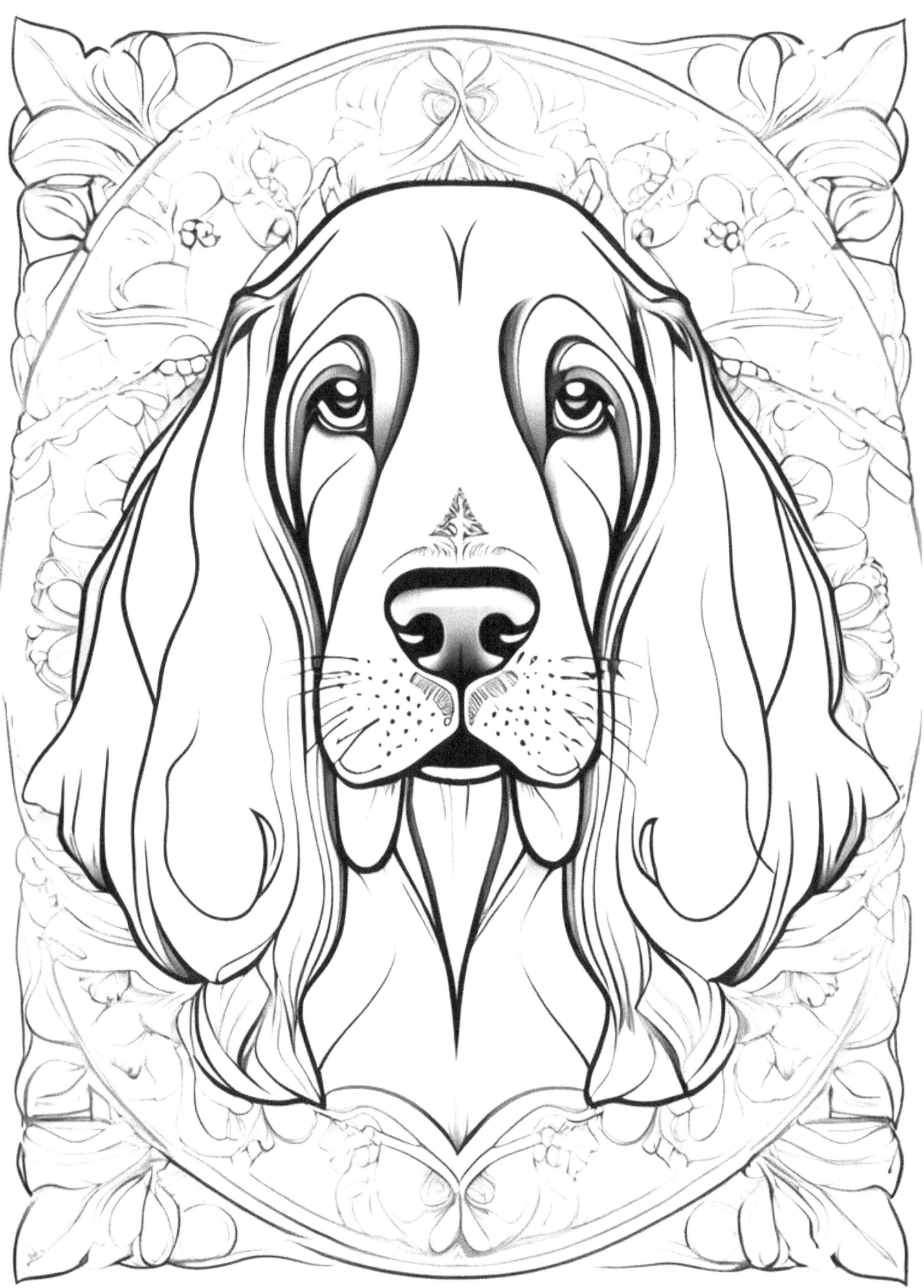

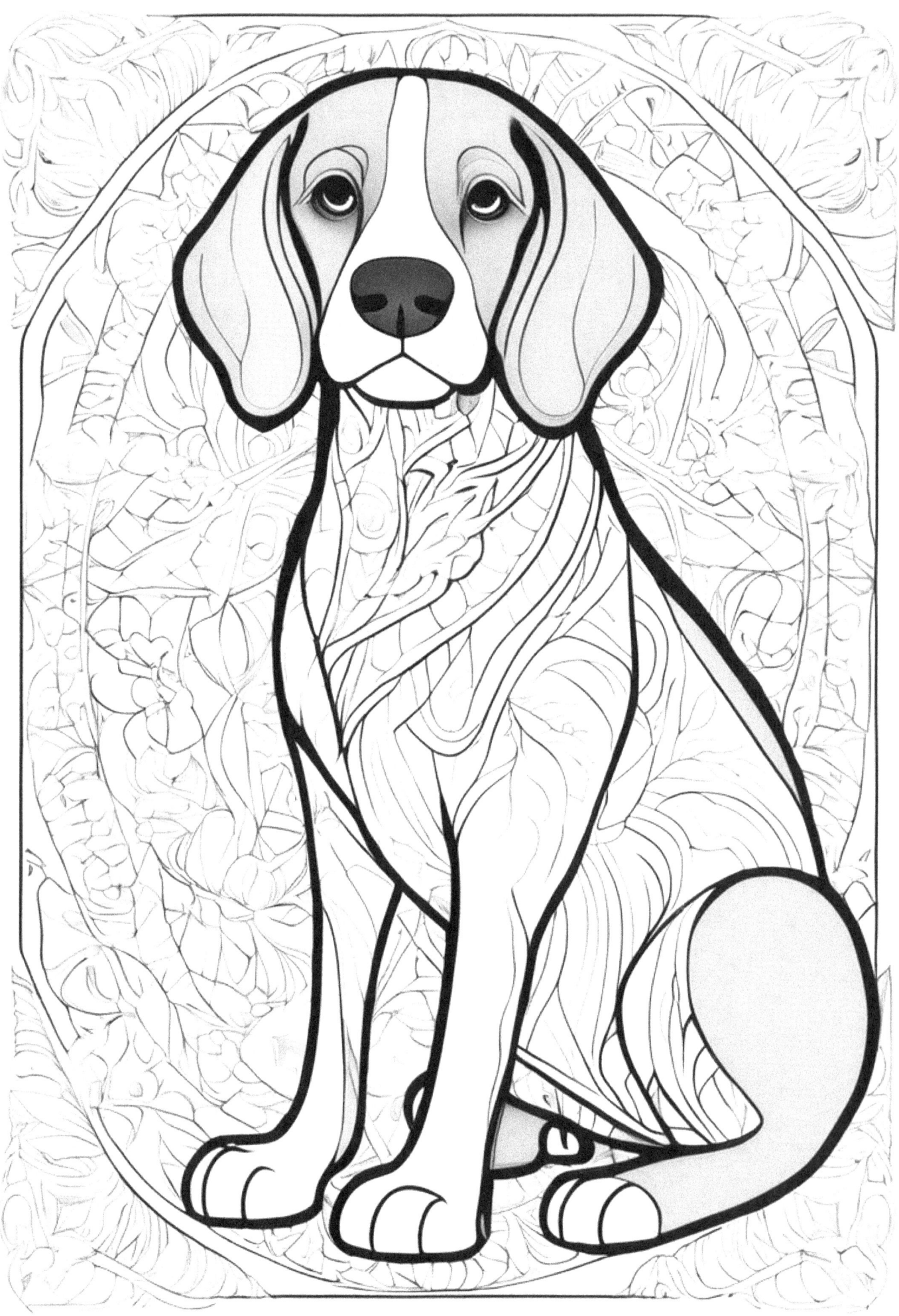

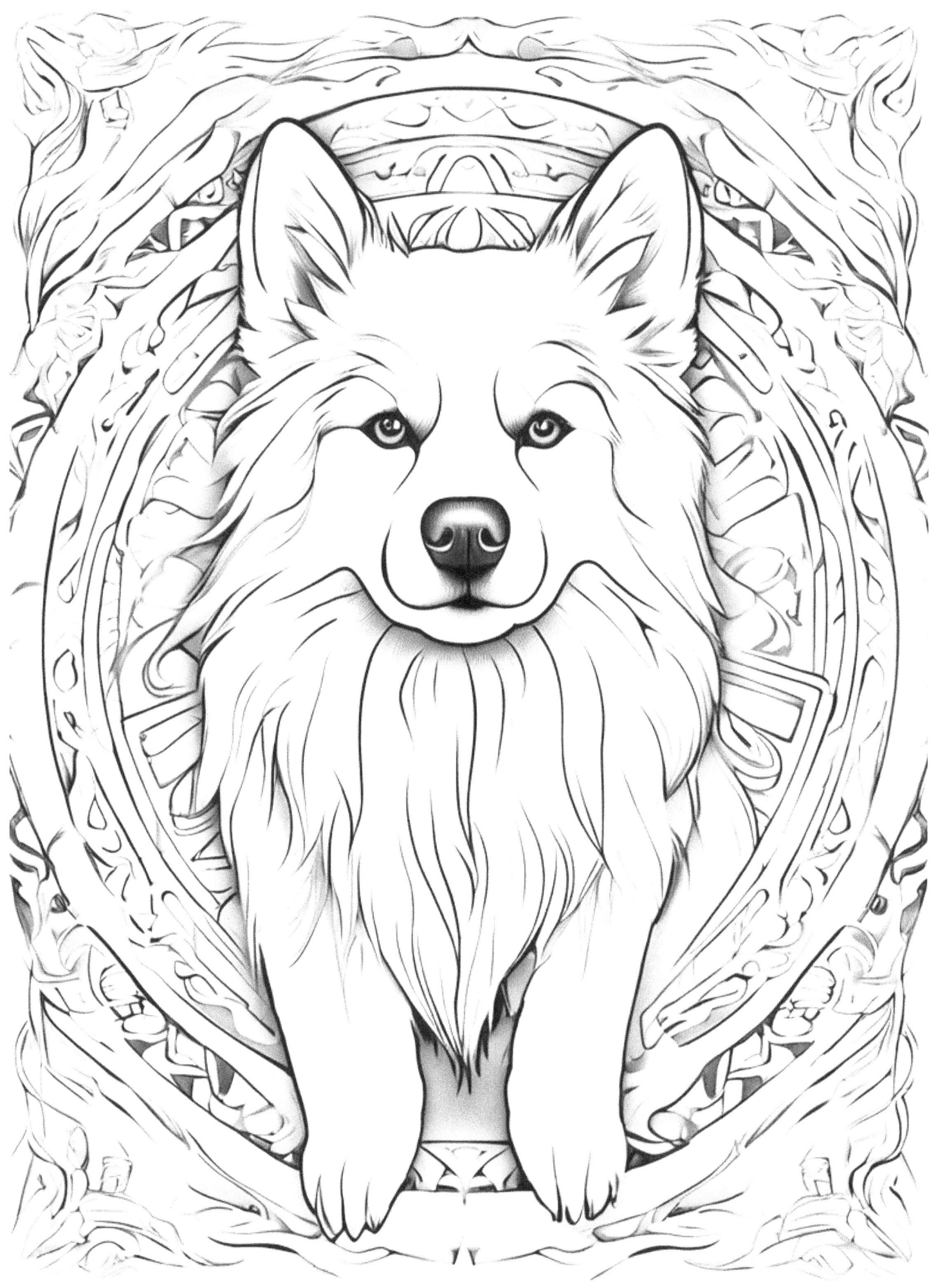

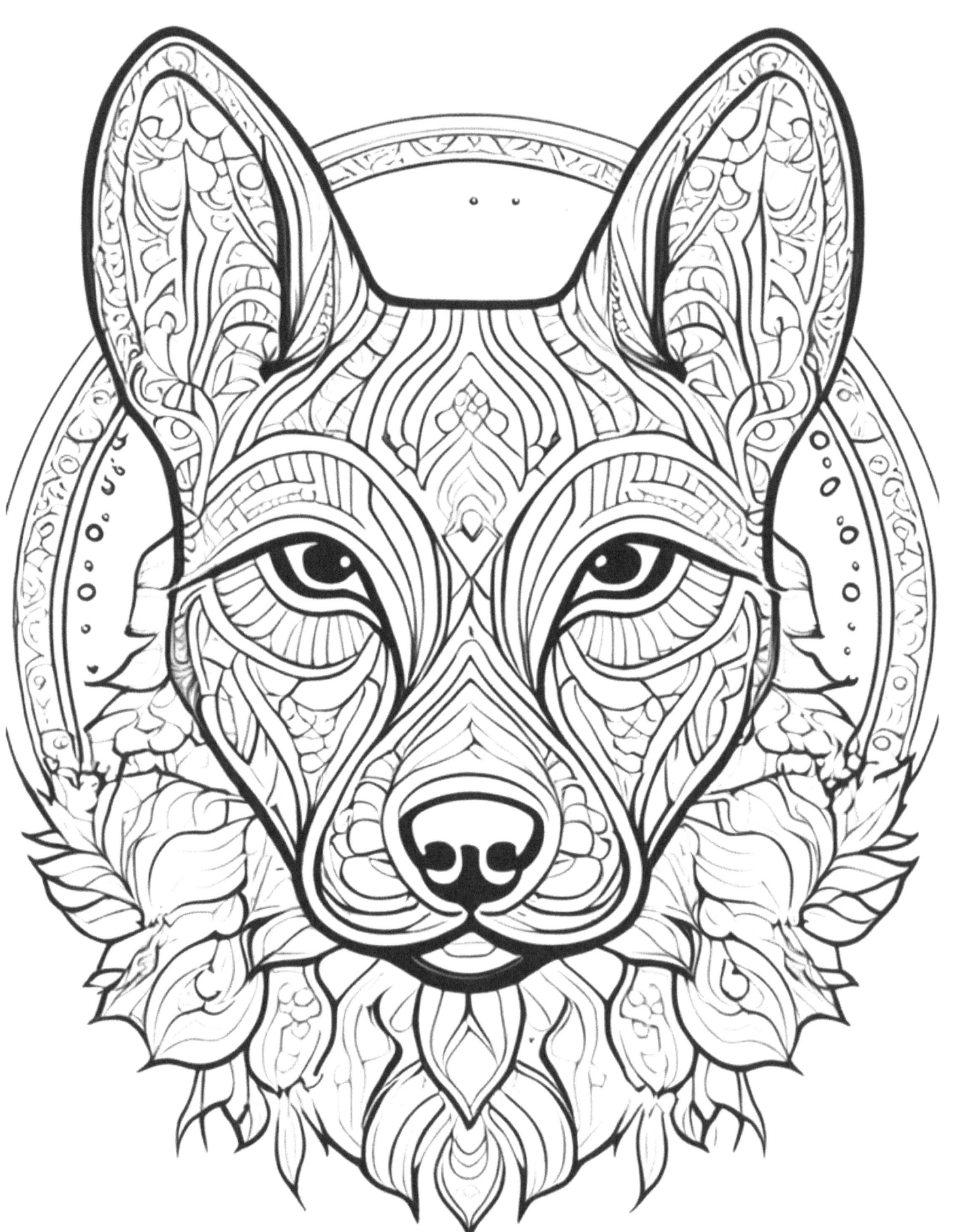

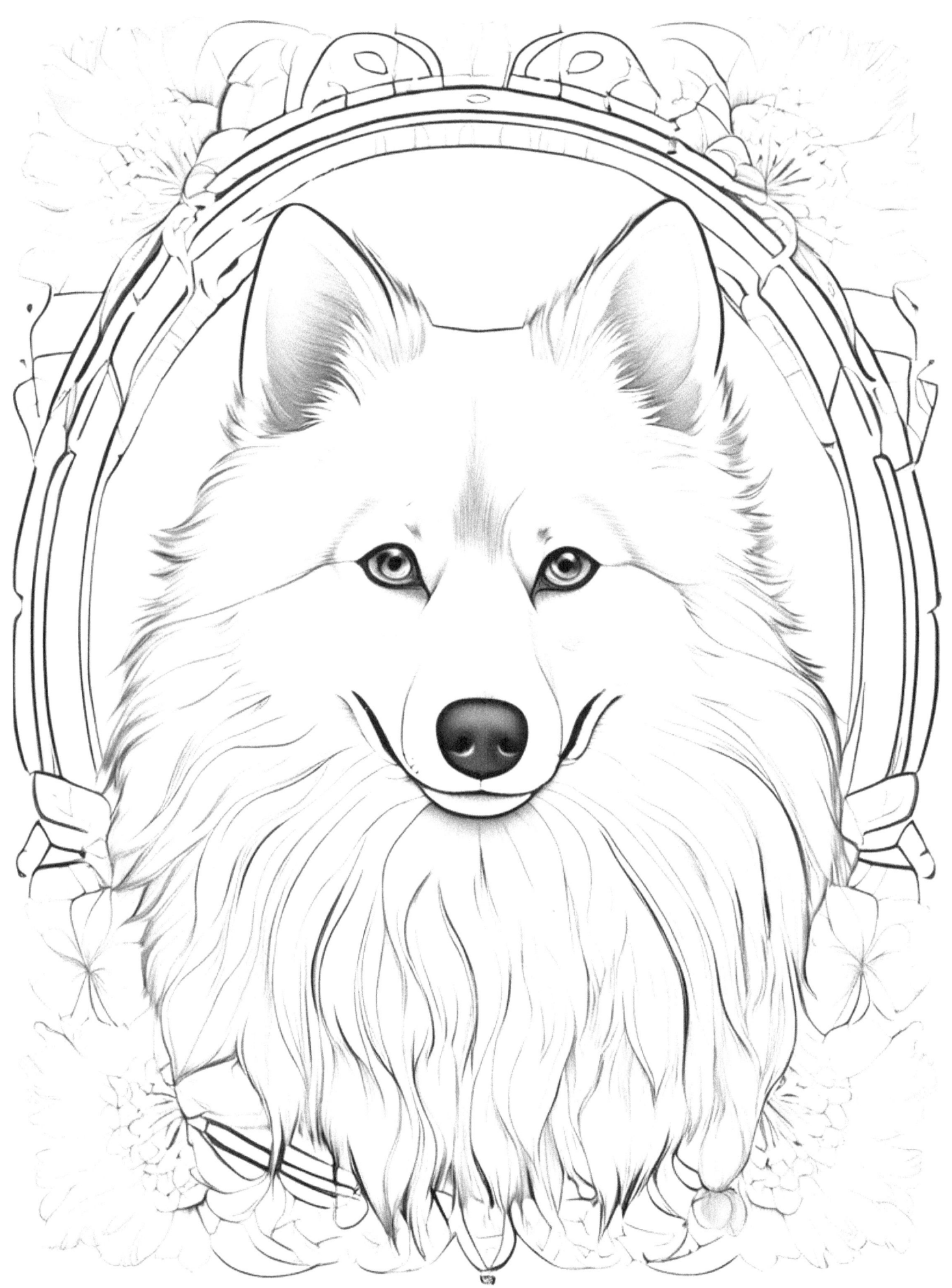

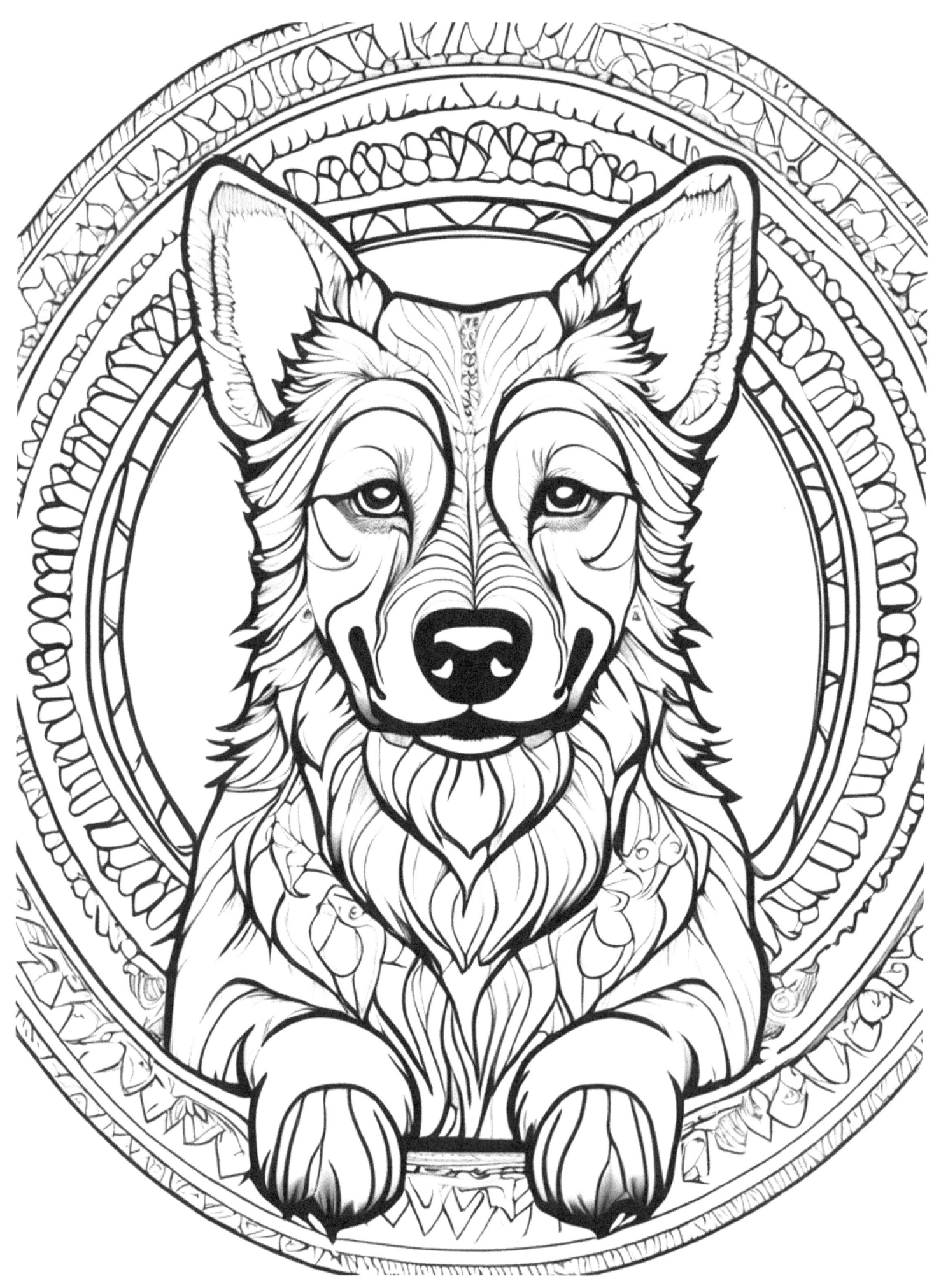

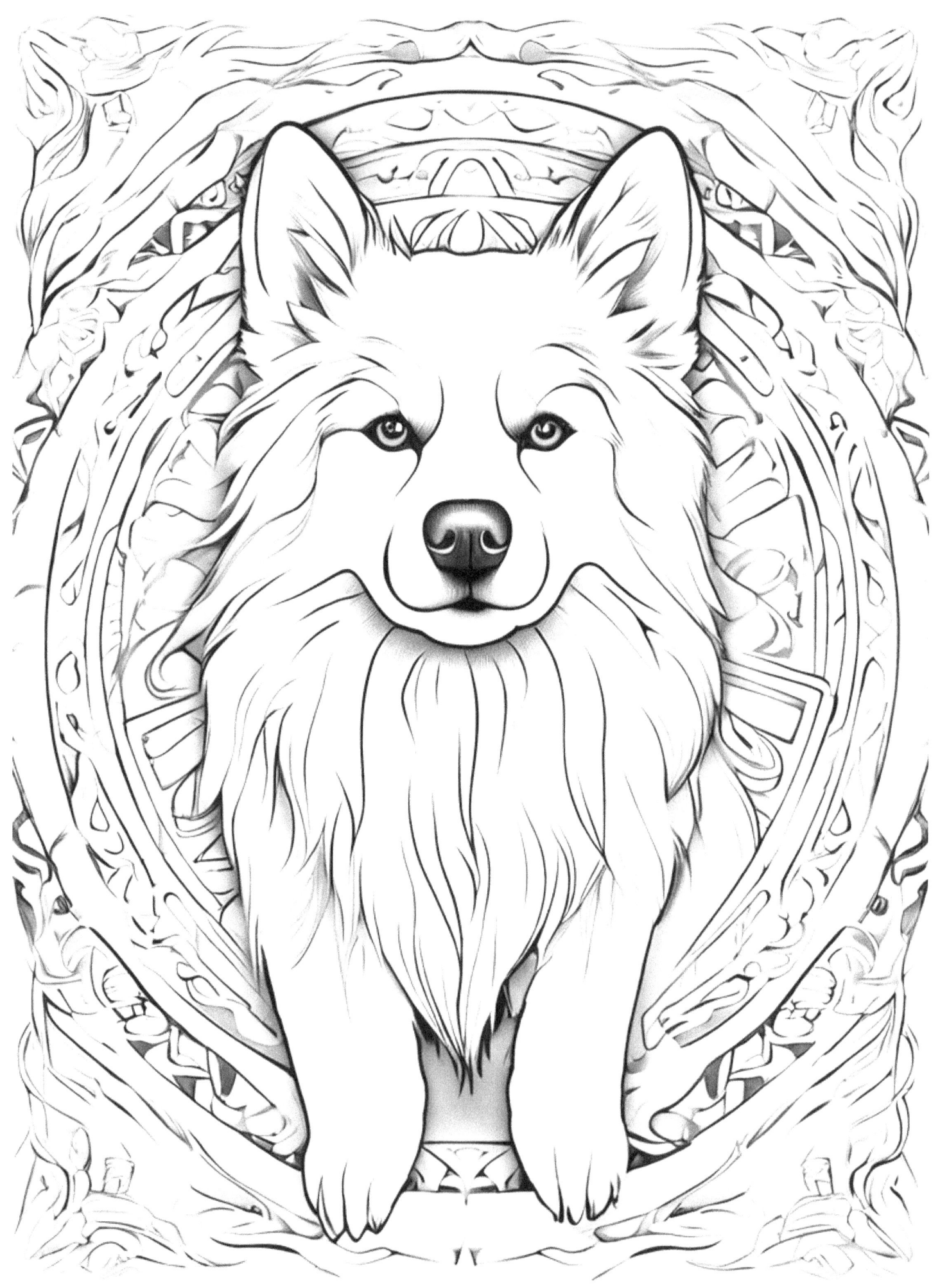

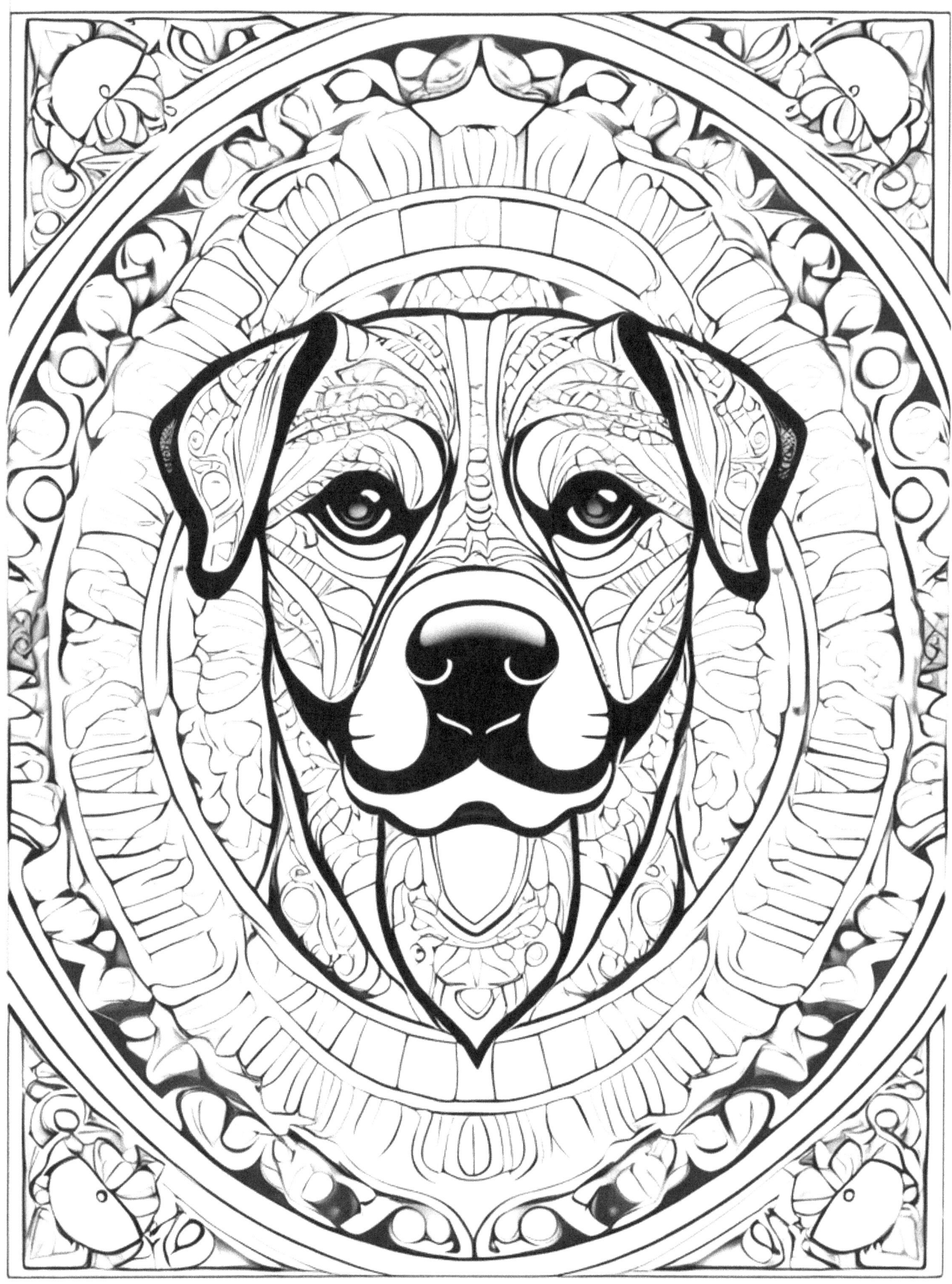

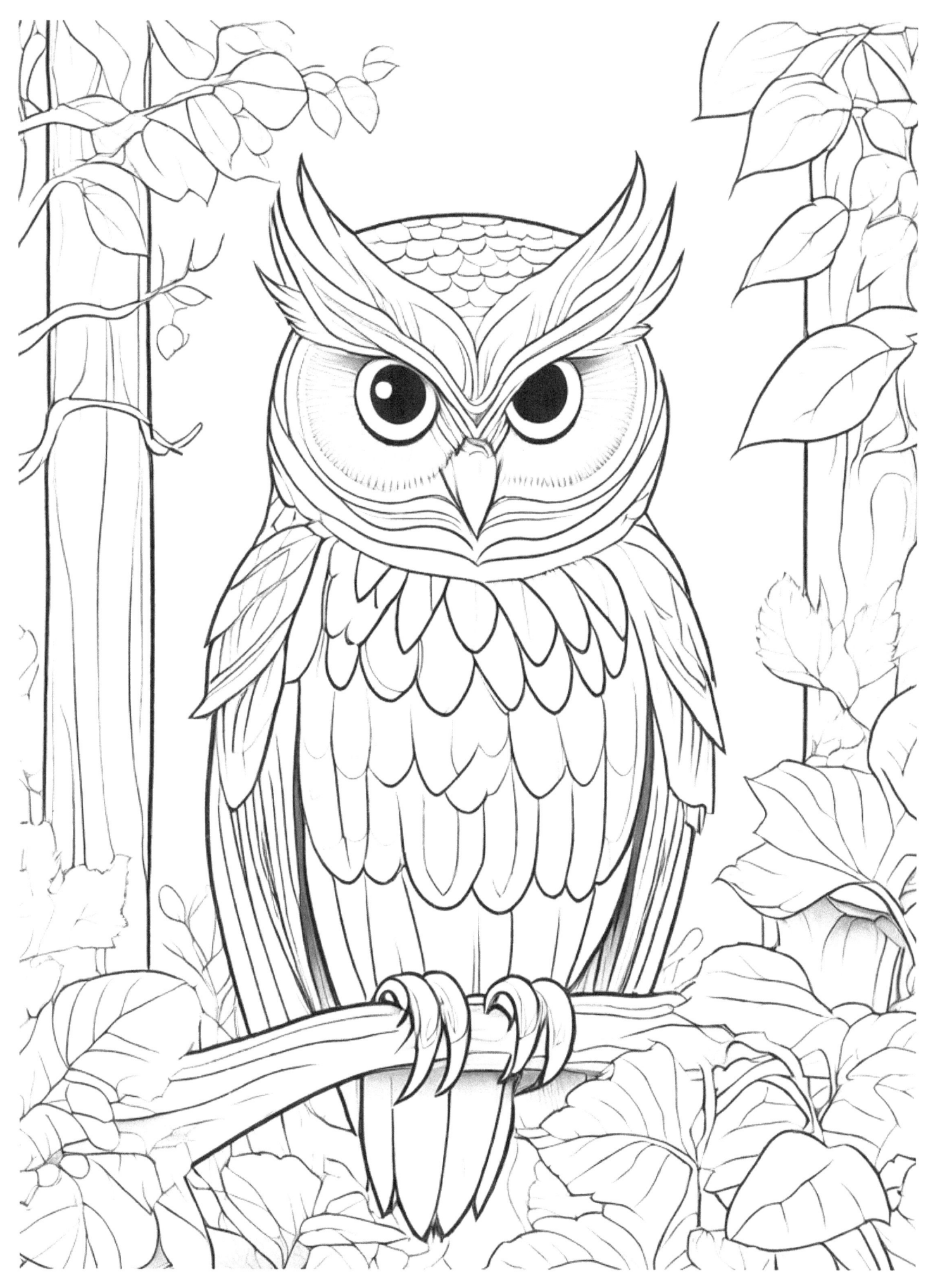

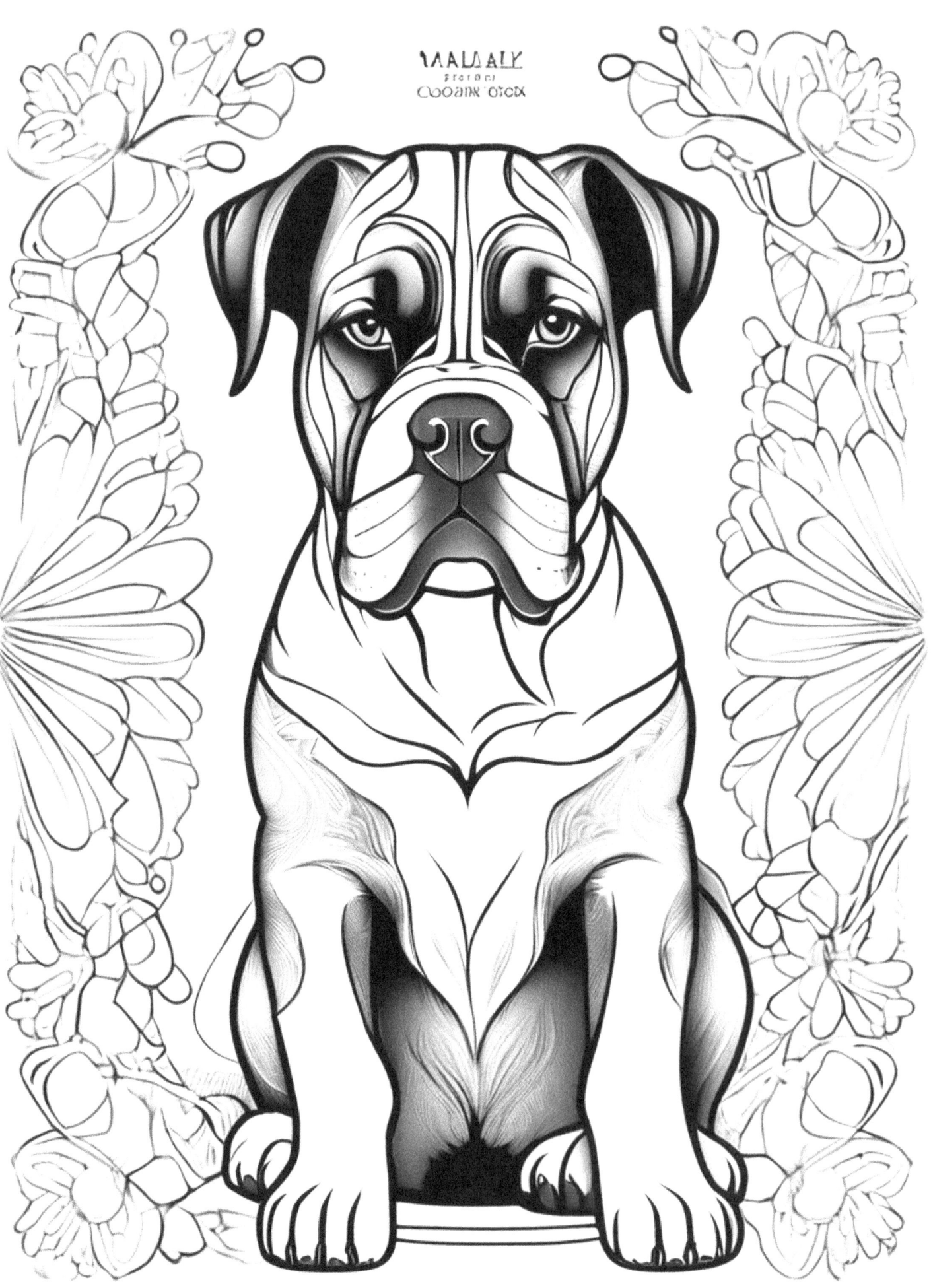

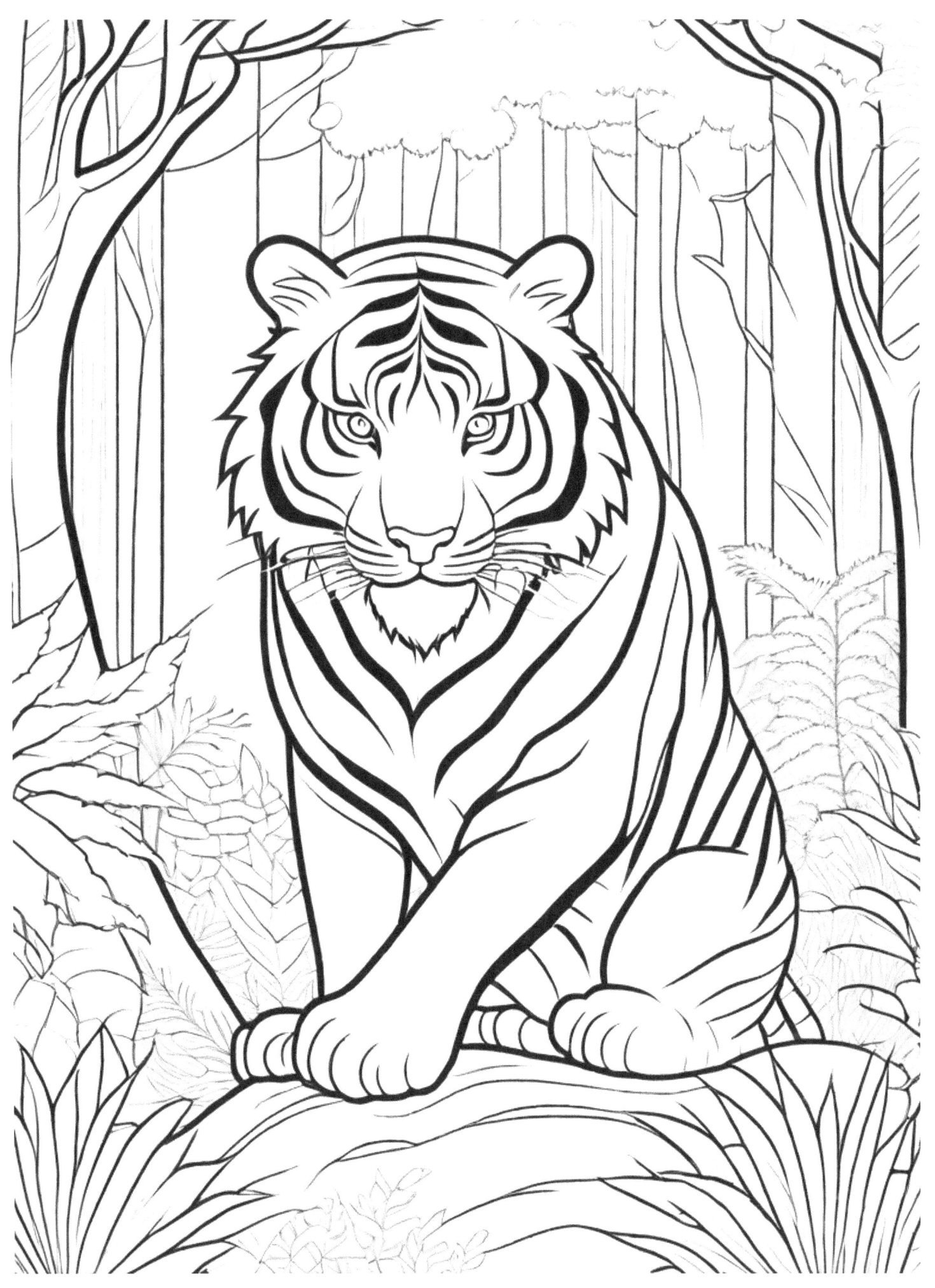

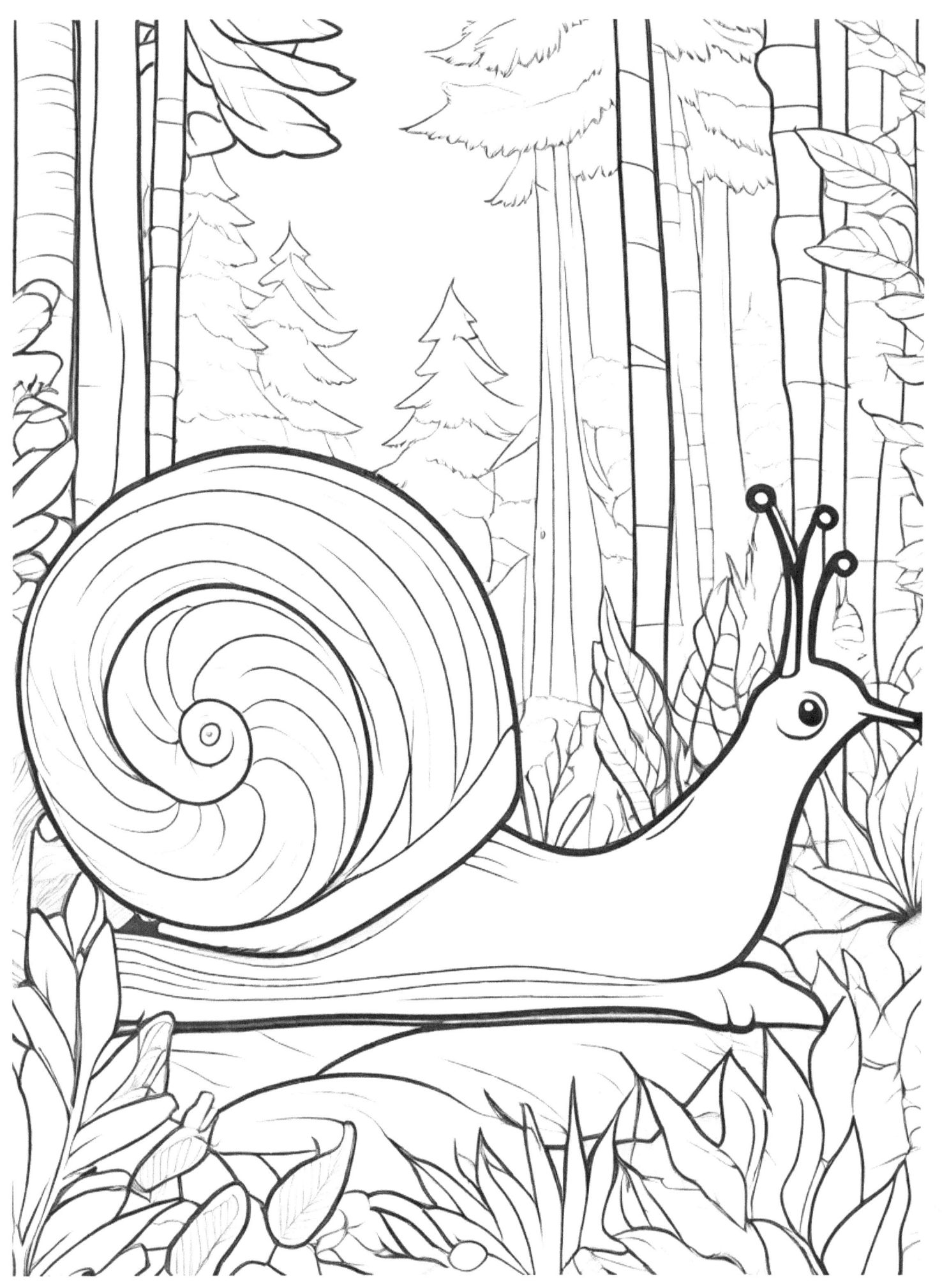

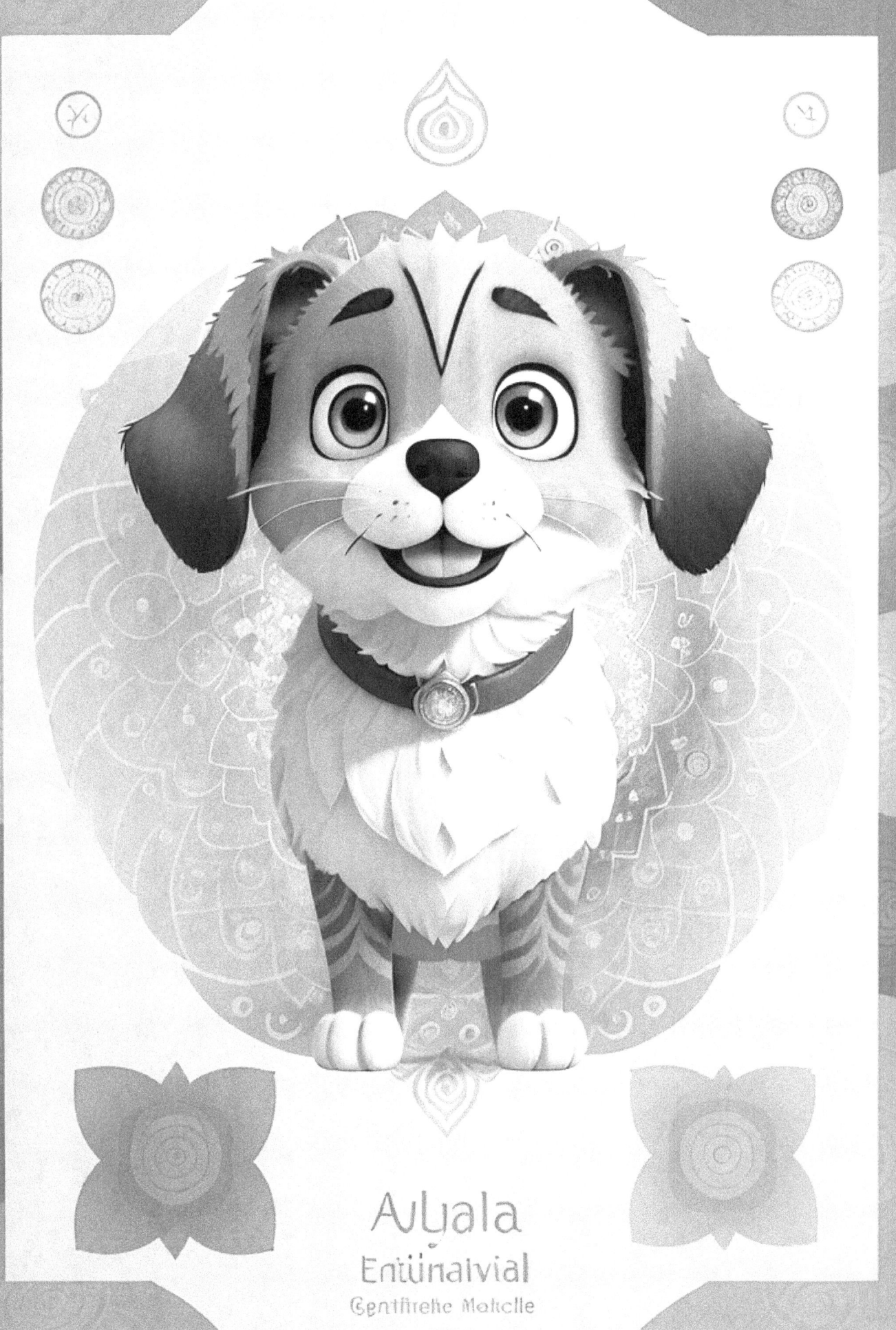

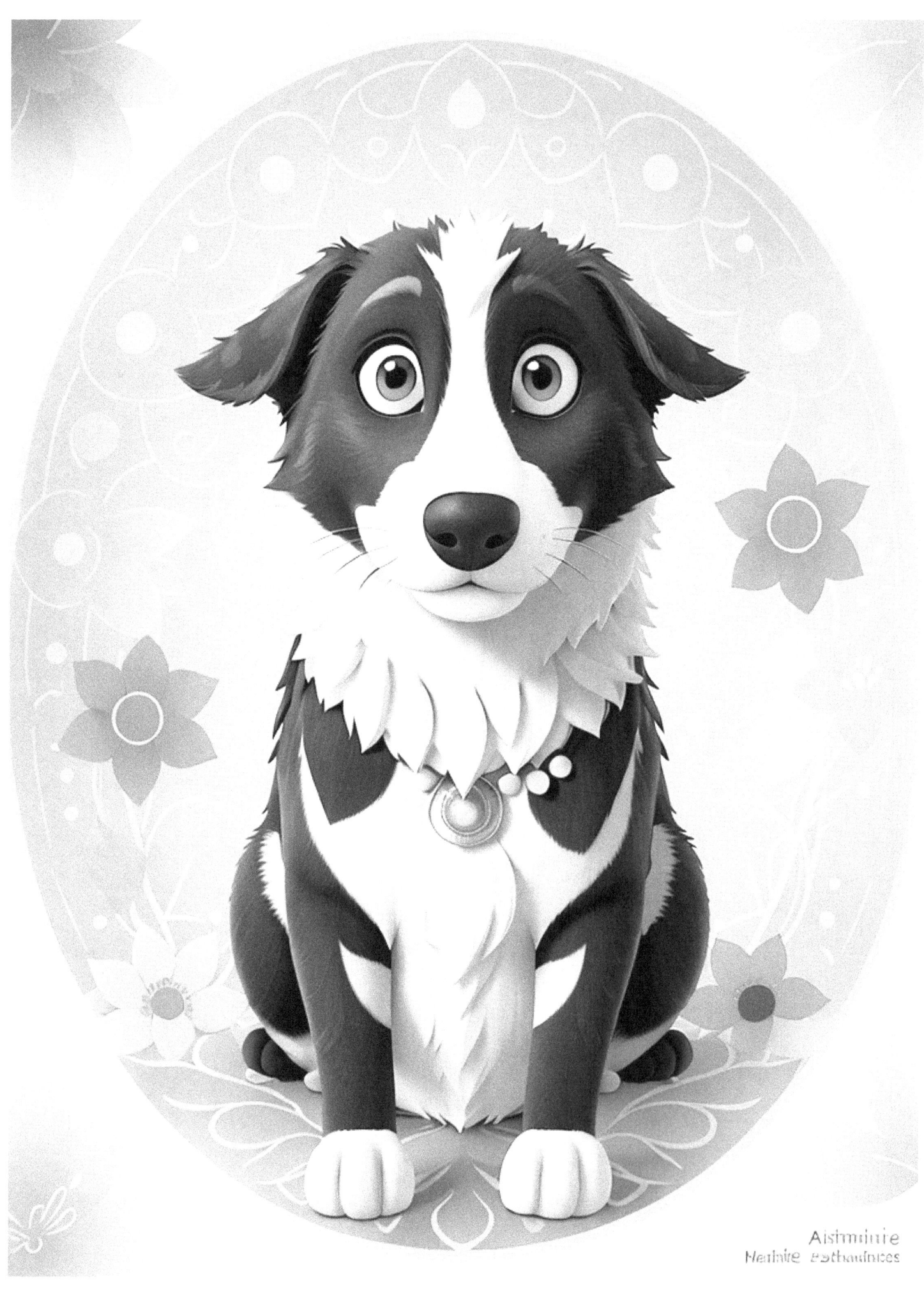